Stra·te·gic Spell·ing

Moving Beyond Word Memorization in the Middle Grades

Jonathan P. Wheatley

Maple Ridge, British Columbia, Canada

INTERNATIONAL
Reading Association
800 BARKSDALE ROAD, PO BOX 8139
NEWARK, DE 19714-8139, USA
www.reading.org

Director of Publications Dan Mangan
Editorial Director, Books and Special Projects Teresa Curto
Managing Editor, Books Shannon T. Fortner
Acquisitions and Communications Coordinator Corinne M. Mooney
Associate Editor Charlene M. Nichols
Production Editor Amy Messick
Assistant Editor Elizabeth C. Hunt
Books and Inventory Assistant Rebecca A. Zell
Permissions Editor Janet S. Parrack
Assistant Permissions Editor Tyanna L. Collins
Production Department Manager Iona Muscella
Supervisor, Electronic Publishing Anette Schütz
Senior Electronic Publishing Specialist R. Lynn Harrison
Electronic Publishing Specialist Lisa M. Kochel
Proofreader Stacey Lynn Sharp

Project Editor Shannon T. Fortner

Cover Design, Linda Steere; Art, www.clipart.com

Library of Congress Cataloging-in-Publication Data
Wheatley, Jonathan P., 1968-
  Strategic spelling : moving beyond word memorization in the middle grades / Jonathan P. Wheatley.
      p. cm.
  Includes bibliographical references and index.
  ISBN 0-87207-559-1
  1. English language--Orthography and spelling--Study and teaching (Middle school) I. Title.
  LB1574.W44 2005
  372.63'2--dc22

Second Printing, November 2005

2005001672

To my family, especially Sandra

con·tents

pref·ace

Many middle school teachers and students are tired of memorized weekly word lists. Both are ready for something a little more thought provoking. This book will help you teach students in grades 5–8 to spell better using an instructional format that is teacher friendly, interesting for students, and effective. Strategic Spelling, the methodology presented in these pages, is built on the belief that teaching language patterns and spelling strategies is more powerful than having students memorize words.

The seeds for this book were planted almost 15 years ago during my first years as a classroom teacher. Everywhere I turned, I got a different perspective on how to teach students in the middle grades to spell better. At first I taught spelling using a traditional word-memorization program. Then I used less formal methods, such as student writing conferences and personal spelling lists. I read many spelling texts, but they seemed out of touch with my daily reality of trying to teach several subjects to 30 students who possessed widely varying abilities. Everything I tried fell short in one way or another. Some approaches were too dry, others merely extended activities that were designed for younger students, and many just required too much teacher preparation and assessment. I wanted to improve my students' spelling, but not at the expense of other subjects.

These early experiences prompted me to search for another way to teach spelling. When I could not find a spelling resource that I felt would hold my students' interest, I began experimenting. I wanted activities that motivated my students to think, analyze, and discuss words more deeply. Over time I realized that the key motivator was not the grades I gave but how I framed the lessons. When I approached spelling activities as games, races, challenges, and puzzles to be solved, my students quickly began talking more positively about words and spelling.

I knew for certain that I was on to something when I heard even my struggling learners making comments such as "This is not spelling; it's fun," and "This hurts my head." I was finally getting students to really think about words! It was clear that they were more interested, challenged, and actively involved using this approach.

Since these beginnings, I have steadily developed, researched, and refined this methodology. As part of my master's of education program, I used the approach to improve grade 6 and 7 students' spelling skills and tracked the results. Students taught with this approach gained significantly greater spelling-strategy knowledge, were better able to spell isolated words, and rated their spelling lessons three times more favorably than students who were taught with more traditional methods (Wheatley, 2000).

In my own school district, this approach has spread rapidly among other teachers. When I present this spelling methodology at conferences and workshops, I hear again and again from teachers who are excited to finally be able to *teach* spelling—in a way that better reflects how students actually learn to read, write, and spell. Both teachers and students appreciate this more active, thoughtful approach to spelling.

Strategic Spelling: Moving Beyond Word Memorization in the Middle Grades has gradually emerged from my classroom and is supported by current research findings. Over the years I have refined the approach based on classroom experiences with students as well as feedback at workshops and discussions with colleagues. The approach takes into account what educators already know about how students learn. It highlights the strategies that good spellers use and discusses the important patterns they notice. Most important, this approach strives to use activities that better capture student interest because to maximize learning we need to engage our students' emotions. We need to do more than simply ask students to memorize words for a spelling test. To truly improve spelling, we need to teach strategies and language patterns in a manner that engages students.

In this book, I provide an alternative approach for teaching spelling in the middle grades. It is intended to be a flexible instructional framework for you to adapt and build on. It is not a prescriptive lockstep program of predetermined words and activities. How you use this approach will depend mainly on the needs of the students within your classroom.

Chapter 1 provides the theoretical foundation for Strategic Spelling. It discusses this approach's four core principles and a range of related research concerning effective spelling instruction and acquisition. This chapter also examines spelling acquisition from a developmental perspective and discusses the role of reading and writing within this process.

Chapter 2 examines how to better incorporate spelling into your curriculum. In this chapter, core spelling strategies are introduced along with an explanation of how to best use this book. An integral part of this discussion focuses on how to ensure you meet the needs of all students, including those with special needs.

Chapter 3 offers a series of Pattern Activities to systematically train students how to use the spelling strategies because "a skill—no matter how well it has been taught—cannot be considered a strategy until the learner can use it purposefully and independently" (Routman, as cited in Kosnik, 1998, p. 60). During the activities, students consciously practice using the strategies that good spellers use unconsciously. To be effective, spelling instruction must teach more than word patterns; it must teach students to use

systematic spelling strategies to accurately spell unfamiliar words (Snowball, 1997; Wong, 1986). The Pattern Activities reinforce strategy use and get students to notice language patterns.

The Thinking Activities in chapter 4 will help you draw student attention to the language patterns that are especially important for this age range: syllabication, affixes, spelling–meaning connections, and changes to vowels and consonants (Bear, Invernizzi, Templeton, & Johnston, 2000; Ganske, 2000). Students work together in small groups to discover key language patterns, using word lists that they generate themselves. The activities may be implemented as individual assignments, but using them as collaborative activities meets some of the social needs of middle school students. The cooperative Thinking Activities counterbalance the individual-student Patterning Activities, and both kinds of activities are taught concurrently.

To make the activities as easy to implement as possible, a consistent outline is used throughout the book. Each activity begins with a brief summary and relevant research connections, followed by the following sections:

Materials lists the materials you will need to have on hand to complete the activity with your class.

Advance Preparation alerts you to any steps you will need to complete before presenting the activity.

Lesson Format includes time required, objective, and step-by-step guidelines you can use as a basis for or extension of your instruction.

Reinforcing the Spelling Strategies highlights the ways in which the activity relates to the spelling strategies and suggests ways to further reinforce strategy use.

Activity Scoring offers a system for scoring the activity with minimum effort.

Teaching Tips offers implementation ideas that you may want to consider or emphasize during the course of the activity.

Special Needs Considerations addresses how you may use the activity to the best advantage with English-language learners and students who have learning challenges.

Extensions to the activities are offered in some cases.

Chapter 5 offers Supplementary Activities to help you better integrate spelling instruction across the curriculum. These classroom-tested ideas connect Strategic Spelling with other reading and writing tasks.

Chapter 6 examines how to assess student spelling knowledge within everyday writing. The multiple purposes of assessment are explored, and the differences among assessments for word knowledge, strategy knowledge, and understanding of language patterns are discussed. Because the time and energy that can be realistically dedicated to spelling assessment are limited in a busy classroom, Strategic Spelling assessment strategies are those that provide the most useful information in the least amount of time.

The book's conclusion offers guidance for continuing to use this spelling methodology within the framework of greater literacy development. Strategic Spelling reproducibles are presented at the end of the book to give you a more practical organizational format for daily classroom use.

With Strategic Spelling, you will help students better understand the importance of patterns and strategies across the curriculum—not just in word spellings. This type of instruction helps students to become more aware of the predictability that exists in other subject areas. It helps them to examine other work in a different light. This emphasis on patterns and strategies has certainly helped me to better focus my daily discussions with students. I hope you find this method and these activities as valuable in your classroom as I have in mine.

Why Teach Strategic Spelling?

The research makes it clear that students in the middle grades *do* need to study words to better understand the English language. They need systematic instruction that helps them to organize their word knowledge (Butyniec-Thomas & Woloshyn, 1997; Moats, 1995). But this instruction needs to be presented in a more integrated and thought-provoking manner in order to help students better understand how words work. Bear et al. (2000) suggest that

> word study at the intermediate level should demonstrate to students how their word knowledge can be applied to advance their spelling knowledge, their vocabulary, and their strategies for figuring out unknown words. At the intermediate and middle grades, the following principles should guide instruction:
>
> • If students are actively involved in the exploration of words they are more likely to develop a positive attitude towards word learning and a curiosity about words.
>
> • Students' prior knowledge should be engaged; this is especially important if they are learning specialized vocabulary in different disciplines or content areas.
>
> • Students should have many exposures to words in meaningful contexts, both in and out of connected text.
>
> • A sequence of teaching about structural elements should be followed: syllables, affixes, and the effects of affixes on the base words to which they are attached. (p. 221)

When competent adults read and write, they do not refer to a set of rules they have memorized. Rather, they recognize new words by comparing them, or the patterns within them, to words they already know (Adams, 1990; Liberman, Rubin, Duques, & Carlisle, 1985; Templeton & Bear, 1992a, 1992b). Students, too, are constantly using patterns and strategies when spelling (Caine & Caine, 1997; Gable, Hendrickson, & Meeks, 1988). These important patterns and strategies are the things that spelling instruction in the middle grades must target more explicitly.

What Is Strategic Spelling?

The methodology in this book is built on four core principles to better match classroom instruction with how students access patterns to spell in the real world:

1. Make spelling instruction more fun and engaging.

2. Increase student discussion, analysis, and thought.

3. Provide explicit instruction and practice with spelling strategies.

4. Increase student awareness and use of important language patterns.

The most important of these core principles is to make spelling instruction more fun and engaging. Traditional word-memorization spelling programs are rated by both teachers and students as the subject they least enjoy (Gentry, 1987). Yet current brain research (Caine & Caine, 1997) indicates that emotions are critical to memory patterning. Clearly, spelling lessons need to become more interesting and thought provoking before students will better retain in their long-term memory the concepts we are teaching. Caine and Caine note that learning is also enhanced by challenging activities and is inhibited by threat. To help students to learn better and to retain what they have learned, Strategic Spelling lessons increase active participation; encourage more group work; and present tasks more as games, challenges, or puzzles.

The second core principle is to increase student discussion, analysis, and thought. By the time they reach the middle grades, students often have deeply entrenched beliefs about how the English language works. Most of these beliefs help them to read and write accurately. In some instances, however, students' beliefs foster poor spelling habits and faulty logic. They might fail to drop or add necessary letters when adding affixes, or continue to overuse letter patterns that are rarely used in multisyllable words (i.e., using the letter *d* alone for past tense rather than *ed*). Strategic Spelling uses activities to push older students to metacognitively examine *how* their thinking has led them to spell the way they do—to think more deeply about their thinking in regards to the strategies they have considered, the patterns they have noticed, and connections to previous knowledge they have made. This is an essential part of spelling instruction. After all, if you do not ask students to examine their beliefs, how can you expect them to change? With this approach, activities such as Word Challenge in chapter 3 encourage students to examine their spelling beliefs by requiring them to include spelling strategies, and evidence that these strategies work, when spelling a selected word.

Students learn most when they are involved in thoughtful discussions with others (Caine & Caine, 1997). Unfortunately, activities that encourage students to collaboratively discover, discuss, and explain important word patterns do not happen nearly enough in traditional spelling instruction. Strategic Spelling provides many opportunities for students to discover, discuss, and reflect on spelling patterns. Throughout the Thinking Activities (chapter 4), students are asked to work collaboratively in small groups to analyze words they generate themselves for key language patterns.

The third principle is to provide students with explicit instruction and practice with spelling strategies to help them become better spellers. Good spellers unconsciously use many spelling strategies, but students often only use spelling strategies that they have been specifically taught (Clark & Uhry, 1995; Ralston & Robinson, 1997). Heavy emphasis on phonetic instruction in the primary years often means that many poor spellers remain overly dependent on sound when spelling challenging words (Moats, 1995). Quick and effective spelling strategies that are not phonetic need to be taught to middle-grade students. Strategic Spelling explicitly teaches other strategies—detailed in chapter 2—so that students are not relying on sound alone. The Pattern Activities in this book (chapter 3) are all designed to provide students with instruction and practice on how and when to use a number of effective spelling strategies.

The fourth core principle of Strategic Spelling is to increase student awareness and use of important language patterns. The human brain seeks out patterns (Caine & Caine, 1997; Levine, 2003). Educators need to more effectively draw students' attention to language patterns that can be helpful for this age range. In the middle grades, many of the most common error patterns occur when students attempt to add or drop letters. For example, students are often unsure about whether to double some letters. A simple pattern that can resolve this confusion is to teach them to split words into syllables. If the word contains doubled letters, then these letter combinations tend to be split across syllable breaks (e.g., *swim·ming, hel·lo*). By explicitly teaching these common patterns, Strategic Spelling provides students with tools to spell correctly not just during spelling class, but also as they are writing. After all, the real goal of examining words with students is to help them "learn how to learn" words so they can read and write competently (Wong, 1986). The Thinking Activities and Pattern Activities are designed to make students more consciously aware of how language patterns, and the connected spelling strategies, can be used to spell more accurately when writing.

Using Strategic Spelling means that even though you are the teacher, you do not have to be a word expert. Instead, you create an environment in which students notice patterns and make connections. When you lay this foundation, students often learn more than the content you are teaching.

What the Research Tells Us About Spelling Instruction

The English language is an amazing system of overlapping and connected patterns. At the alphabetic level, word spellings are highly variable because students still rely almost completely on sound to spell. They think in terms of one-to-one letter-to-sound correspondence (e.g., *bat* = /b/-/a/-/t/; three letters = three sounds), and they are still relatively unaware of how letters can work together to create sounds (e.g., the *o* and *a* work together to create the long /o/ sound in *boat*). They are equally unaware of how important word meaning and word history can be when spelling. For example, the word *musician* uses a *c* rather than an *s* because of its spelling–meaning connection with *music*, and it has historically used only a *c* rather than a *ck* to make the ending /k/ sound. When letter patterns, meaning, sound, and word history are considered together, however, the English language is over 80% predictable (Bouffler, 1997; Zutell, 1998).

Traditional spelling texts have teachers spend a great deal of time administering tests, marking activities, and discussing definitions that label words (e.g., *antonym, synonym, noun, verb, adjective*). In such lessons, underlying lan-

guage patterns and spelling strategies do not get enough discussion and analysis. These texts require students to memorize words without regularly reviewing the spelling strategies that could help them (Westwood, 1999). Richard Gentry (1987) says these word-memorization approaches teach "dead symbols with no bridge between facts and...experiences" (p. 5). Compounding this problem is the fact that teachers themselves are not always aware of all the strategies they unconsciously use to spell (Kosnik, 1998). Word-memorization approaches have perpetuated the belief that spelling is a boring and difficult task; however, there are much better ways to teach spelling.

Spelling Acquisition From a Developmental Perspective

The human brain is always searching for connections, always looking for ways to understand the environment. The brain acts in the same manner when students are learning to read and write. The brain notices and uses letter patterns of increasing complexity as students advance in reading ability. In spelling acquisition, the process of gaining complex pattern recognition and use can be viewed as a series of developmental stages that begins in the preschool years and continues into adulthood.

Children rely primarily on sound. As they age, they begin to use other sources of information. Good spellers effectively use sound, visual cues, meaning, and kinesthetic knowledge (Moats, 1995). As students become better able to use all this information, they progress through five developmental spelling stages:

1. **Emergent:** Children begin to write strings of letters or letter-like figures, but there is no connection between the letters written and their alphabetic sounds. In this stage, children are not yet reading.

2. **Letter Name:** Students rely on sound to spell, and they think in terms of one-to-one letter-to-sound correspondence (e.g.,

sit = /s/-/i/-/t/; three letters = three sounds). They have begun to read, can understand the concept of a word, and often write at least the beginning and end consonants of simple words.

3. **Within Word Pattern:** Students can spell most single-syllable, short-vowel words correctly. They have also developed some sight words, correctly use a number of consonant blends and digraphs, and are learning about long vowels. When reading, they have moved from decoding text letter by letter to reading short words and phrases.

4. **Syllable Juncture:** Students can spell most single-syllable words accurately. They are learning how to consistently add, drop, or double letters when spelling multisyllable words. Students can read fluently and have automatic word recognition of most high-frequency words.

5. **Derivational Constancy:** Students realize that because of the underlying meaning in a word, the spelling of its root can remain constant across several related words, despite changes in pronunciation. In this stage, students spell most words correctly, read fluently, and notice connections between related words.

These five developmental stages can be divided into approximate age and grade ranges (see Table 1). By the middle grades, the majority of students in any classroom are functioning in the Syllable Juncture and Derivational Constancy stages (Ganske, 2000; Templeton, 1992b). In these last two stages, students are effective readers and writers. Instruction is primarily focused on reinforcing and expanding their language understandings. At this point, the syllable has become the most important unit for processing language. For middle school students, most errors occur when students double or drop letters where syllables meet (Bear

et al., 2000; Henderson & Templeton, 1986; Schlagal, 1992).

Syllable Juncture Stage. In the Syllable Juncture stage, students spell most single-syllable words accurately but are still learning some of the patterns in multisyllable words. Most spelling issues in this stage revolve around what happens at syllable junctures when affixes are added or removed; for example, students often struggle with knowing when to double letters where syllables connect. Many ending consonants need to be doubled when a suffix is added (e.g., *skip/skipping*); with silent *e* words, however, the ending consonant must remain single to maintain a long vowel sound (e.g., *rope/roped*). So when students learn about when to double or drop letters at syllable junctures, they are also developing a better understanding of related patterns, such as how long- and short-vowel patterns influence spelling.

Henderson (1990) suggests the two most important concepts for students to grasp at this stage:

1. A short vowel indicates that the consonant is doubled (e.g., *bag·gage, ca·ter·pil·lar,* and *set·tle·ment*).

2. The silent *e* is dropped when adding suffixes (e.g., *compose/composition, mobile/ mobility,* and *preserve/preservation*).

In addition to these two concepts, instruction that reviews how long and short vowel sounds influence syllable breaks is helpful:

1. In words with long vowels, syllable breaks consistently fall after the vowel (e.g., *cra·zy, be·lieve*).

2. In words with short vowels, syllable breaks regularly fall after the consonant (e.g., *sil·ver, fun·ny*).

Bringing attention to these simple patterns can go a long way in helping middle school students become better spellers.

Derivational Constancy Stage. Once students progress through the Syllable Juncture stage, they enter Derivational Constancy. In this stage, students realize that many words are spelled in a similar manner because they are derivatives of a common root. Some students reach this final stage of development as early as grade 4, but most arrive during grade 7 or 8 (Ganske, 2000). In this stage of spelling development, students continue to expand their personal spelling systems. The stage lasts through high school and postsecondary education (Anderson, 1985; Gentry, 1982).

The three most important concepts for students to grasp at this stage are as follows:

1. Words with similar meanings often have similar spellings.

2. Consonants and vowels interact to change the way multisyllable words sound. (This is especially true when prefixes and suffixes are added to roots, for example, *locomote/locomotion*.)

3. Words are influenced by their history. Often a word's history can be traced back to the meaning of an ancient root. Many modern-day words contain Greek or Latin roots that influence their meaning.

Students overcome remaining spelling difficulties by taking advantage of the connections among related words. They learn to notice that many related words have similar spellings; for example, students use their knowledge of the word *inform* to help them spell *informant*, *information*, and *informative*. By making the spelling–meaning connection, students come to understand that words that do not sound the same may still be spelled in a similar manner (e.g., *derive/derivational*).

Connections Among Spelling, Reading, and Writing

Views about how spelling should be taught stretch along a continuum. At one end are those who believe that spelling skills are best learned incidentally while students engage in authentic reading and writing. At the other end are those who believe that instructional time needs to teach specific spelling skills in a structured and sequential manner. Research indicates that balancing these two approaches is likely the most effective way to optimize spelling growth (Butyniec-Thomas & Woloshyn, 1997).

The bulk of the words students learn are picked up incidentally while they read and write (Henderson & Templeton, 1986; Smith, 1988). The average adult can read, write, and spell 50,000–70,000 words. Spelling texts can only present 4,000–6,000 words (Henderson & Templeton, 1986). This means that any instructional approach to spelling is only one part of a broader literacy program.

For most students, extensive reading—not additional spelling instruction—is the surest way to improve spelling competency. This is because students are quickly exposed to a significant number of words in a meaningful context when they read. Routine exposure to frequently used words and letter combinations enables

Table 1. The Five Spelling Stages (Age and Grade Ranges)

Developmental Spelling Stage	Age Range	U.S. Grade Range
Emergent	1 to 7	pre-K to mid-1
Letter Name	4 to 9	1 to 2
Within Word Pattern	6 to 12	2 to 4
Syllable Juncture	8 to 12	3 to 8
Derivational Constancy	10 and up	5 to 8+

Adapted from Ganske (2000). Grade-level ranges refer to the point at which at least one-third of any class will be operating within the developmental stage.

students to recall language patterns more easily (Geekie, Cambourne, & Fitzsimmons, 1999; Kosnik, 1998; Moats, 1995). Spelling acquisition is a continuous and unconscious process whereby students create new spelling understandings by expanding on existing knowledge (Bouffler, 1997; Buchanan, 1989; Gentry, 1987; Krashen, 1989). The students who read and write the most, then, are the ones who develop understanding about how words work: "Spelling knowledge grows out of and supports reading, writing, and vocabulary study. It also grows out of examining words in and of themselves" (Templeton, 1992a, p. 455).

The relationship between reading, writing, and spelling is highly interconnected. Numerous studies have found high correlations among reading comprehension and decoding ability, vocabulary level, and spelling competency (Ehri, 1989; Honig, 1997). Frequent writing also encourages spelling development because students are able to "see" if their words look right (Laminack & Wood, 1996; Tarasoff, 1990). Stephen Krashen (1989) described the effect of reading and writing on spelling as the input and output hypotheses. The input hypothesis proposes that most language acquisition occurs incidentally as students read for meaning. The related output hypothesis suggests that language is also learned through writing when students actively confirm or contradict their word spellings. Together, reading and writing significantly improve students' spelling acquisition.

We need to continue to emphasize meaningful reading and writing activities throughout the curriculum. Spelling instruction in the middle grades is an important component of meaningful reading and writing activities when it helps students to notice useful patterns, connections, and strategies. There are just too many words, too many rules, and too many exceptions for any student to realistically memorize. Good spellers mentally reconstruct words using letter patterns (Goswami, 1992; Liberman et al., 1985; Templeton, 1992a). Students need

to learn exactly how to use this same process: "The use of strategies and the knowledge of patterns go hand in hand—they help make English less confusing and provide students with the tools to use when spelling" (Kosnik, 1998, p. 62).

The human brain instinctively uses patterns. Humans apply what they know about familiar words to new ones (Caine & Caine, 1997). The importance of applying pattern knowledge as you decode a passage is graphically demonstrated in the reading of this terribly misspelled message, forwarded to me by a colleague:

> Aoccdrnig to a rscheearch at an Elingsh uinervtisy, it deosn't mttaer in waht oredr the ltteers in a wrod are, the olny iprmoetnt tihng is taht the frist and lsat ltteer is at the rghit pclae. The rset can be a toatl mses and you can sitll raed it wouthit porbelm. Tihs is bcuseae we do not raed ervey lteter by itslef but the wrod as a wlohe. Amznig! (author unknown)

In this message, the beginning and ending letters of every word are accurate. This predictability allows the brain to unscramble the remainder of the word. The brain constantly uses patterns (including prefixes, suffixes, and roots) to decipher shades of meaning and to compose deep understandings of words. This means middle school students must be taught how to both recognize word patterns and apply systematic spelling strategies, including how to

- simplify words by looking for consistent word parts,

- listen for smaller words within longer ones (because the spelling of shorter words and word segments often remains constant),

- pronounce words to cue their auditory memory,

- separate words into syllables, and

- think about related words (because words with similar meanings often have similar spellings).

Good spellers use all of these spelling strategies at one time or another. It's essential that students come to know these strategies so they can apply them in real-world reading and writing situations. When students read, write, and spell, they are constantly being exposed to numerous overlapping patterns. To make use of all of these patterns, they must consider more than just how a word sounds. Breaking a word down into syllable sounds, or considering the phonetic patterns embedded within them, is a good spelling strategy. It cannot be the only strategy, however, because the spelling of many words is influenced more by meaning than sound.

The Syllable as Perceptual Unit. The syllable is the main perceptual unit used by people when they read and write (Bouffler, 1997; Templeton & Bear, 1992b; Zutell, 1998). In fact, the two most common types of spelling errors made by middle school students occur at syllable junctures. These are the points where individual syllables meet. Students are often unsure about when to double or drop letters at these syllable junctures (Bear et al., 2000; Henderson, 1990; Schlagal, 1992). This means that instruction that targets developmentally appropriate skills (such as syllabication and segmentation) can go a long way toward helping students in the middle grades read, write, and spell better.

The Increasing Importance of Nonphonetic Patterns. The concrete nature of phonics makes it a tempting basis for middle school spelling instruction. In the primary grades, there is no doubt that phonics is a crucial building block in learning to read. But for most middle-grade students, emphasizing phonics does not lead to improved spelling accuracy. In fact, overreliance on phonetic strategies is a common characteristic of poor spelling ability (Radebaugh, 1985). As words become more complex, nonphonetic patterns (including word meaning and word history) play a greater role in spelling. The increasing importance of these nonphonetic patterns means that phonics is a less reliable spelling strategy for multisyllabic words (Henderson, 1990; Templeton, 1992a).

The limits of English phonetic patterns are demonstrated dramatically in an experiment in which a computer was programmed with every phonetic rule and then asked to spell 17,000 words (Hanna, Hanna, Hodges, & Rudorf, 1966). Even with perfect phonetic recall, the computer only managed to spell 49% of the list words accurately. Spelling by sound alone is not reliable. To spell accurately, students need to be taught to consider visual patterns and spelling–meaning connections as well as sound (Westwood, 1999).

Spelling instruction is only worthwhile to the degree that it helps students notice and exploit patterns. By embedding explicit spelling instruction in your own classroom's rich reading and writing opportunities, you maximize learning not only in spelling but also in reading and writing as well.

Spelling as an Active Thinking Process

Spelling involves more than just simply matching sounds with letters. It is a highly intellectual process that involves the use of a number of strategies and the coordination of several sources of knowledge (Graham & Miller, 1979; Henderson & Templeton, 1986; Kosnik, 1998; Wong, 1986). It is not enough for students to recite language patterns (e.g., "*i* before *e* except after *c*"); students need to actively examine them. To maximize learning and retention, students must think more deeply about the English language. They need to spend ample time discussing word patterns, examining the connections between words, and learning the strategies that good spellers use. In order for students to effectively use pattern knowledge and spelling strategies, they must have general problem-solving competence (Gerber, 1982). The process of learning how to read, write, and spell is more of a thinking process than a memorization task.

Middle-grade students are ideally suited to developing observation and critical thinking skills. At this age, students have developed the cognitive abilities necessary to fully understand many of the important patterns that make multi-syllable words predictable. They can also learn to analyze words for sound, visual, and meaning patterns. They can be taught that most multisyllable words ending in the /shun/ sound are spelled with the ending *tion*. They can be trained to notice that *able* attaches to roots that are already stand-alone words (e.g., *size + able = sizable*), while *ible* attaches to roots that are not recognizable words by themselves (e.g., *poss + ible* or *vis + ible*). They can be shown that many words have similar spellings because they have similar meanings (e.g., *real, realistic, realize, reality, realization*).

Students go through a major developmental shift at about grade 5, a shift that allows them to use analogy to more efficiently recall and examine words. For example, a student unfamiliar with the word *plantation* could most likely deduce its spelling because he or she probably knows the root word (*plant*), can hear the /a/ sound, and knows that many multisyllable words ending in the /shun/ sound are spelled with the ending *tion*. Researchers (Adams, 1990; Templeton, 1992a; Wolff, Desberg, & Marsh, 1985) believe the ability to use analogy does not appear much before this time because younger students have not yet acquired enough word knowledge to make sense of analogies. In the context of spelling instruction, this newly acquired cognitive ability allows students to better analyze, compare, and predict word patterns based on previous knowledge: "As students become increasingly aware of spelling patterns and their applications, they can better predict the structure of unknown words" (Westwood, 1999, p. 27). Vygotsky (1978) calls the relationship between learning and cognition the "zone of proximal development." This "zone" is the place where instruction succeeds in actively developing the "ripening" mental functions of students. To stretch students' cognitive abilities, you can ask them to complete tasks that they cannot do alone but that they *can* complete when provided with structure and assistance (Geekie et al., 1999). By having students apply newly acquired thinking skills, such as analogy, you help them

recognize common language patterns and use strategies they may not have considered on their own. By routinely comparing and contrasting words, observing and interpreting word patterns, summarizing what they notice, predicting patterns, and applying a variety of spelling strategies, students become better spellers.

Incorporating critical-thinking skills into lessons is nothing new in most subjects. Professional texts actively promote greater use of problem-solving strategies in science, math, social studies, and reading. Isn't it about time that spelling also be taught in a manner that matches students' cognitive abilities? Many of the Pattern and Thinking Activities in this book require students to more actively compare, contrast, interpret, and summarize information than traditional word-memorization approaches. They ask students to make more connections between words being examined and what they already know about language patterns and spelling strategies.

The Role of Student Attitude and Motivation in Spelling Instruction

The classroom climate is as important as anything else in students' learning environment (Laminack & Wood, 1996). Teaching students to spell well is more than just instructing them in a series of skills; it is about helping students develop a positive attitude. Attitude plays a fundamental role in learning.

Middle school students need lessons that engage them, that ask them to collaborate with their peers, and that clearly show how patterns and strategies help them read and write. Middle school students do not remain cognitively or emotionally engaged if instruction is about rules and assignments are artificial tasks. By the middle grades, students are tired of the weekly-word-list routine. In the words of one of my former students,

> Last year spelling was boring because all you did is take tests. First you take a test that doesn't matter,

and then you take one that does. All you do is learn how to spell words you forget anyway. (Rochelle Doran, grade 7)

Students enjoy the novelty, challenge, collaboration, and logic of the Strategic Spelling approach. The jobs of discovering patterns, analyzing words, and working through activities that are framed as challenges are refreshing to them. To hold student interest, use the three 4-letter words that always motivate students: *game*, *race*, and *food*. These three motivators appear throughout the activities because they consistently energize students. As one former student of mine wrote,

> Keep doing the hard words in spelling. Memorizing words is just plain boring. I'm so glad you understand. (Sheila Isaaks, grade 6)

Sheila's comment is indicative of one of the biggest differences between the Strategic Spelling approach and traditional word-memorization approaches: the delivery. Traditional spelling programs do not do enough to actively engage older students or to provide teachers with a sense that they are actively teaching spelling. Comparatively, Strategic Spelling shows students how specific, concrete strategies and visible language patterns can help them to become better spellers, readers, and writers. This distinction was not lost on another student, who said,

> You know, with spelling lists you don't get the meaning very much. (Mirko Carich, grade 7)

Mirko made the connection that words with similar meanings have similar spellings. He also realized that he had not really considered this connection when he was being taught spelling with traditional methods. This realization is significant; for students to be able to consistently spell larger words, they need to grasp the spelling–meaning connection.

Strategic Spelling balances individual work and collaborative work. This balance maximizes the learning of middle school students who need thoughtful interaction with others (Caine & Caine, 1997). Many of the Thinking Activities are best taught as cooperative lessons in which students rely on each other. The benefits of cooperative instruction include increased time on task, improved one-to-one discussion, and improved student self-esteem. Plus, some students will just plain like each other better once they have worked together a few times (Johnson & Johnson, 1987; Slavin, 1990). From a metacognitive perspective, group activities help students to make connections they may not make working alone (Rosencrans, 1993). In fact, one review of 70 quality cooperative-learning studies found that in only one study did traditional teacher instruction produce greater achievement than lessons utilizing cooperative learning strategies (Slavin, 1990).

In the middle grades, learning is a social process that works best through discussions with peers, problem solving, and meaningful literacy experiences (Rosencrans, 1998). Regularly incorporating these interactive features into your instruction improves students' ability to pay attention, which is significantly linked to their attitudes about learning. How you influence your classroom climate is as important as anything you teach: If the students aren't interested, what you are trying to teach doesn't matter.

This chapter has provided a research-based rationale for changing the way spelling is taught in the middle grades. There needs to be greater emphasis placed on pattern and strategy instruction. Strategic Spelling is built on four core principles to more explicitly develop spelling skills that can be used quickly in realistic writing situations. This approach provides a solid foundation to better understand spelling's developmental nature and places this information within a larger literacy context. Chapter 2 will build on this theoretical base by examining core spelling strategies and discussing how to best incorporate this approach into your classroom.

chap·ter 2

How to Incorporate Strategic Spelling Into Your Curriculum

As discussed in chapter 1, by the middle grades, students are ready for you to explicitly teach many language skills, including significant letter patterns, meaning connections among words, and other strategies that good spellers use. Students can be taught to better notice significant letter patterns, such as when to use *ei* or *ie*. In this example, students can be trained to notice that most *ei* words make the long /a/ sound, and most *ie* words make the long /e/ sound. They also can learn to better use spelling–meaning connections so they are not fooled into spelling words such as *critic* and *criticize* differently because of differences in sound. They can be shown how to better use strategies such as syllabication to help decide whether a word should have one or two of a letter (*des·sert* versus *de·sert*). Students in the middle grades are ready to more critically examine how language patterns and spelling strategies relate to their own knowledge of phonics, syllabication, rhyme, affixes, and spelling–meaning connections. When you implement Strategic Spelling in your own classroom, you will notice an improvement in both your students' attitude and spelling skills. This focus on significant letter patterns, meaning connections among words, and other strategies that good spellers use is the basis for Strategic Spelling. It provides students with a framework to make better sense of word patterns.

When combined with daily reading and lots of authentic writing opportunities, the Strategic Spelling activities increase student awareness about how words are constructed. Strategic Spelling helps to highlight important patterns that allow students to approach challenging words more strategically. For example, students will learn to notice that the word *unintelligible* is made up of smaller words that they can hear (*in* and *tell*); contains two *l*'s, which are split by the syllable break (*tel·li*); and possesses both a common prefix and suffix. Because *intellig* is not a stand-alone word, students will also know that the suffix *-ible* starts with an *i* and not *a*. You can use Strategic Spelling as a comprehensive, yearlong spelling methodology or simply as a complement to existing spelling curriculum. With this methodology, you will

- improve students' ability to notice and exploit language patterns;
- challenge students to think about why words are spelled in particular ways;
- enable students to develop concrete spelling strategies that can be used in all situations; and
- introduce spelling concepts in a fun, interactive, and engaging manner.

All of the activities in this book were designed with the intellectual and social skills and needs of middle school students in mind. The activities work best in grades 5–8, but they can also be used successfully with slightly younger students when appropriate teacher support is provided. Strategic Spelling provides tools to help students better understand word patterns and spelling strategies. The activities are flexible enough to be used in a traditional spelling period or integrated in other subjects. You can easily apply the methods in novel-study units, social studies or science vocabulary discussions, or in word-study opportunities that arise in other subjects.

Strategic Spelling is an engaging, cognitively challenging, general-purpose approach to spelling instruction. It is not an intervention program for students with special needs. Special considerations for students with learning challenges are noted in the activities.

That said, most spelling errors made by students who have learning challenges are similar in nature to those made by other students (Worthy & Invernizzi, 1990). The significant difference is that students with learning challenges may function at an earlier stage of spelling development. Most special needs students integrated within my own classrooms have functioned at the Within Word Pattern stage or higher. Strategic Spelling's emphasis on patterning and strategies has enabled many of these students with special needs to successfully complete the assigned activities at their own level of functioning. They have benefited from classroom activities that have emphasized group work, vowel sounds, syllabication, spelling strategies, and affixes. Strategic Spelling cannot, however, be the only spelling instruction students with special needs receive. They also require additional instruction targeting their specific areas of need. For students with special needs in my own classroom, this has often meant additional remediation focused on long- and short-vowel patterns, syllabication, high-frequency words, and affixes and their related add/drop letter patterns. With all students, however, the focus is still the same: Provide predictable patterns and spelling strategies to highlight the logic of the English language.

Students who find school difficult often have poor pattern recognition (Levine, 2003). Such findings suggest that appropriate classroom spelling instruction can make a significant difference if it emphasizes important language patterns and strategy instruction.

Spelling difficulties arise from a variety of sources. There may be underlying problems with language, cognitive processing, visual processing, memory retention, phonological processing, or learning strategies. Difficulties may also be the result of inadequate instruction (Fulk & Stormont-Spurgin, 1995). Spelling difficulties need to be addressed in ways that are appropriate for the individual student. But, in addition, there are a few things you can do that will help many struggling spellers, whether or not they have special needs. The following sections will guide you in working with students with diverse learning needs.

Helping Students Who Have Mild to Moderate Learning Difficulties

Most classroom teachers do not have the time, resources, or expertise to diagnose the exact causes of every learning difficulty. Fortunately, we do not always need to know the exact causes of a language problem in order to help. Through careful observation, we can often determine what will work. By watching our students in the classroom, we see their strengths and weaknesses: what will motivate them, what they can do independently, what they can accomplish with teacher or peer assistance, and where additional support can be most successful. These daily observations are more useful than a score on any test.

When teaching, our daily observations help refine, adapt, and modify instruction to better meet the needs of all learners. In any lesson, what is more appropriate for some students will be less appropriate for others. The trick is to find that instructional balance where the most students benefit. Finding this balance often means subtly changing lessons to better meet the varying ability levels within the classroom.

Remediating Reading/Spelling Difficulties

When refining lessons for students who have difficulties with reading, it is important to remember that the most effective way to retain information is to change the way the information is presented. Good thinkers cognitively do more with the information they receive than do their peers (Caine & Caine, 1997; Levine, 2003). They more easily notice patterns and are better able to connect what they are learning with what they already know. These cognitive connections help them to more efficiently place into long-term memory the information they receive. Students who have learning challenges may have more difficulty than their peers making connections with their prior knowledge and actively processing information (Moats, 1995). This means that you need to explicitly teach students how to make connections and actively process information.

Base your instruction on high-order thinking to enable struggling students to cognitively rework information they read. Teaching involves more than telling. You must also ensure that you have asked your students to think about, and apply in some manner, what you have taught. By tapping into their high-order thinking skills (through comparing, contrasting, categorizing, hypothesizing, interpreting, and summarizing) you help students retain spelling information in long-term memory. Provide lots of practice in patterning and critical thinking skills, which are emphasized throughout Strategic Spelling, to help your students who have difficulty recognizing patterns.

The Strategic Spelling activities and spelling strategies have been used successfully with many students who have reading difficulties. The explicitness of the strategies and the concrete nature of the activities make sense for many struggling learners. Of course, adaptations may be required, depending on the activity and individual student. Most students with special needs, however, can complete the activities with additional, specific direction and extra support. Work with these students to achieve instant recognition of letter combinations. This skill often translates into accelerated reading progress (Gunning, 1995).

Remediating Writing/Spelling Difficulties

In their written work, students who have special needs tend to include little detail and depth of analysis. Specifically, they may have difficulty identifying and explaining language patterns, and may be less able to connect what they've learned with previous knowledge (Westwood, 1999). You may need to adapt writing activities for students and provide additional instructional support (Graham & Harris, 1994; Moats, 1995; Westwood, 1999).

Extra review of language patterns is especially important for students with learning challenges in terms of their writing. They often possess phonological skills that are weaker than those of their peers and use a smaller range of spelling strategies (Moats, 1995). These limitations can prevent them from making connections between letter patterns and sounds (Goswami, 1992; Read & Hodges, 1982). Provide explicit instruction and direct teaching of a range of spelling strategies to help students gain a fuller understanding of language patterns so that when they write, these students have some concrete tools to help them express their ideas more accurately (Gentry & Gillet, 1993). Emphasize syllabication, long vowels, short vowels, concrete spelling strategies, adding/removing affixes, and spelling–meaning connections in your instruction, as these skills often lead to significant gains in students' written spelling. In addition, offer instruction using word families that share similar letter combinations (e.g., *lace/face/grace*).

In addition to teaching students about patterns, teach them how to select spelling strategies for specific writing situations. The Pattern Activities give students practice using key spelling strategies. *All* students benefit from spelling strategy instruction; students with learning difficulties especially benefit because they do not always see language patterns readily.

General Tips for Working With Students Who Have Special Needs

When teaching, we must always be aware that many students with learning difficulties are already struggling with language or active working memory problems. To help them be more successful, consider the following when teaching:

- The delivery of instructions can influence the degree of difficulty in any task. Ensure that your instructions are not too fast or too detailed.

- Deliberately break down verbal instructions into smaller steps.

- Repeat key words or phrases.

- Provide lots of visual cues that students can refer back to.

- Circulate more frequently near the desks of these "at risk" students.

- Regularly check to ensure they are on task.

- Check for comprehension by privately asking them to explain what needs to be done.

- Adjust the amount of time or the number of questions they need to complete to ensure that the task is something they can realistically complete.

- Adapt assignment assessment criteria to better match with students' academic abilities.

Fair does not always mean equal. We need to be aware that students with learning difficulties often require additional supports that other students may not need. Minor adaptations, such as the ones listed above, involve little extra work but can have a huge effect on how successful our most "at risk" students will be.

Helping Students Who Have Moderate to Severe Learning Difficulties

Sometimes a student's needs are so great that an individualized spelling program is necessary. Using patterned or high-frequency word lists that increase students' sight-word vocabulary is one such option. Teachers in the primary grades commonly use these kinds of word lists to build core vocabulary, automaticity of recall, and language-pattern knowledge (e.g., recognition of long and short vowels).

There are many types of word lists (refer to Cunningham, 2000; McCracken & McCracken, 1993). The type of word list you use depends on the nature of a student's difficulties. If the difficulties are phonetically based, reviewing phonetic patterns may be a good starting point. For example, there are many common phonetic rhyming patterns that can be reviewed, such as the short /a/ vowel sound (e.g., *ham, ram, jam, clam, slam, cram, tram*). In other situations, a review of high-frequency words may be more appropriate; for example, a list of the "100 Most Frequently Used Words" represents about half the words anyone ever uses when writing! There are many high-frequency word lists (see Gunning, 1995; Kosnik, 1998; Westwood, 1999). When selecting materials, keep in mind that the goal is to make students actively think about the way words are being built at their developmental level.

Use the Spelling Strategies Diagram (Reproducible 1) to help make tasks predictable for students. Explicitly teaching critical thinking skills, language patterns, and spelling strategies is effective for all students; however, to be successful, students who have moderate to severe learning disabilities also need intensive instruction and practice.

Helping English-Language Learners

The Thinking Activities and Pattern Activities detailed in the following sections are appropriate for English-language learners (ELLs), provided students are able to understand and complete most grade-level assignments. As long as students can read and write fairly independently, they will be successful because the activities emphasize decoding strategies. Special considerations for ELLs are noted in the activities.

ELLs who operate in early developmental stages (such as Letter Name or Within Word Pattern) will find the activities too complex. In these earlier stages, students are expending a great deal of mental energy just to learn the building blocks of decoding (e.g., long vowels, short vowels, consonant blends, and syllabication). They have not yet developed the sophistication to understand many language patterns, including words within words, consistencies of affixes, and spelling–meaning connections. Additional instruction in reading, phonetic patterns, and high-frequency sight words is more beneficial for students operating in these earlier developmental stages.

How to Use This Book

Spelling Strategies

Research indicates that middle school students benefit from using visual information to determine spelling, in addition to syllabication, rhyme, and meaning, to overcome English language irregularities (Henderson, 1990; Rosencrans, 1998; Templeton, 1992a). The Spelling Strategies Diagram (Reproducible 1) helps students learn how to spell strategically using a problem-solving approach. With this diagram, students can work through spelling difficulties independently. Instead of telling students how to spell a word, you can empower them by asking the questions "What patterns do you notice?" and "What strategy could you use?"

Introducing Students to Using Spelling Strategies. Use direct instruction with the Spelling Strategies Diagram and the Pattern Activities, such as Expanding Words, Rhyme Time, Word Association, Scattered Syllables, and Prove the Pattern provided in chapter 3, to introduce students to using spelling strategies. You don't need to use any particular approach or word list. Use a common text as the basis of your discussion. As long as your class is actively working with the strategies, they will be learning and able to complete subsequent spelling activities. When using the strategies with middle school students, assume that a long word is three or more syllables and a short word is one or two syllables.

"Most of the Time if a Word Looks or Feels Right, It Is!" Spelling proficiency is connected to visual memory capacity (Gentry & Gillet, 1993; Westwood, 1999). In other words, people stop writing when a word they have written doesn't look right. Students can often point out words that are incorrect even when they do not know the correct spelling (Tarasoff, 1990). The visual memory and the sound of words are the two main ways literate adults recall written language (Moats, 1995). By about age 11, students rely on visual information as much as phonetic patterns (Moseley, 1997). They begin to notice the consistency in the roots of related words, and many of the patterns that influence how affixes are added (Templeton, 1992a).

When spelling instruction focuses on rules and exceptions, it may unintentionally undermine students' confidence in their innate spelling abilities. By beginning at the top of the Spelling Strategies Diagram with "Most times, if a word looks or feels right, it is!" you reinforce students' natural tendency to notice and use patterns. When editing with students, I have often found that they can quickly locate misspelled words when asked. In circumstances where students legitimately cannot find a misspelled word, or when they quickly say it all "looks right," it may be necessary to be more direct. In these situations, you select a problem word and ask students to prove that their spelling makes the most sense. Inquire about what strategies and evidence can help to show that their spelling is likely the best. Such approaches help students to more deeply consider what patterns make words look right.

Still Unsure? Choose Your Strategy. Teach students that when a word doesn't look right, they can use spelling strategies to find the right spelling. Systematically review the five strategies with students, using concrete examples.

1. **Rhyme:** Most middle school students naturally use rhyme. It's an effective strategy for working with short words and suffixes. Students make a list of similar-sounding words and then quickly compare the words to determine the correct letter pattern to use. For example, the spelling for a word such as *glint* can be quickly checked by creating a rhyming list of similar-sounding words, such as *hint, tint, dint,* and *print*. Students can use this strategy either orally or as a written list.

2. **Syllables:** Because the syllable is the main perceptual unit used when reading and writing long words, it is an effective tool for spelling. Teach students the four basic guidelines for breaking words into syllables:

   1. Words often break into syllables between double letters (e.g., *shal·low*).

   2. Every syllable has a vowel.

   3. Syllable breaks consistently fall after long vowels (e.g., *cra·zy, be·lieve*).

   4. Words with short vowels break after a consonant (e.g., *sil·ver, fun·ny*).

The syllables strategy works well with long words. Have students divide the word into syllables; then have students determine whether or not the word should have a double letter (e.g., *spel·ling, to·mor·row*).

3. **Word-in-Word:** Students do not always realize that small words embedded in long ones often retain their sound and spelling. Ask students to systematically decode difficult words by breaking them into manageable spelling units (e.g., *forbidden* contains the smaller words *for, bid, den*).

4. **Spelling–Meaning Connection:** This strategy is an extension of the word-in-word strategy. Ask students to consider the connection between spelling and meaning in such words as *ear, hear,* and *heard*. Many words that are connected in meaning are spelled similarly.

5. **Different Spellings:** Using this strategy, students visually check to see if a word looks like it is spelled right by writing down all the possible spellings. Have students use this strategy when they are unsure about just a couple of the letters in a word (e.g., Which looks right: *tommorow* with two *m*'s, or *tomorrow* with two *r*'s?). You'll be amazed at how often students can accurately say if a word looks right.

Have students practice each strategy on their own. Students learn best when they alter the information they receive in some way and make it their own (Caine & Caine, 1997; Levine, 2003). Allow your class to actively "play" with each one prior to assigning tasks that will be evaluated. This will ensure that your students have had ample time to fully understand how each strategy works. You will then be able to confidently assess how well your students apply each of the strategies and not whether they understand how each works. The five strategies can be performed quickly by students in realistic writing situations, but students will use the strategies to differing degrees. Initially, most students rely on the rhyme, syllables, and different spellings strategies because they are taught so well in the primary grades. With practice, however, students soon begin to notice roots and become more comfortable with word-in-word and spelling–meaning connection. Of all the strategies, spelling–meaning connection takes the longest to develop because it is the most cognitively challenging. It is also the strategy most worth promoting; it helps students make sense of multisyllable words.

These five spelling strategies comprise the practical nuts and bolts of the Pattern Activities (chapter 3), Thinking Activities (chapter 4), and Supplementary Activities (chapter 5)—all of which reinforce or expand the five strategies. The activity guidelines are not meant to be static lesson recipes. They are templates to be redesigned and expanded by you. Combine the activities with your own ideas to best reach the students in your classroom.

Correct Spelling/Use a Dictionary. After students have gone through the five strategies, some may still feel that they have not spelled a word correctly. At this point, students may want to use a dictionary. This step, shown at the bottom of the Spelling Strategies Diagram, requires students to halt the writing process in order to physically check a word spelling; therefore, it is not categorized as one of the spelling strategies, which can all be done quickly as part of the writing process.

Spelling Activities

Kosnik (1998) has argued that there are 10 essential components to a rich, interactive spelling program:

1. regular and adequate time,

2. an emphasis on spelling patterns,

3. instruction of concrete spelling strategies,

4. links with reading,

5. links with writing,

6. regular use of helpful resources (e.g., computers and dictionaries),

7. cross-curricular connections,

8. teaching about how the English language has developed,

9. the use of games, and

10. regular use of student reflection.

The Pattern Activities, Thinking Activities, and Supplementary Activities presented in the following three chapters incorporate all of these essential elements.

Pattern Activities

Effective spelling instruction equips students with both an understanding of word patterns and a set of systematic strategies (Snowball, 1997; Wong, 1986). In Strategic Spelling, the enclosed Pattern and Thinking Activities work together to achieve this goal. The Thinking Activities provide students with instruction about the most important language patterns. The Pattern Activities provide students with repeated opportunities to apply Spelling Strategies to word patterns. Try to keep a balance between them, but do not feel that they must be followed in lock-step progression. Curriculum works best when it is responsive to students, so the way you use activities should depend on your classroom's needs (Laminack & Wood, 1996).

The 10 Pattern Activities will help you to teach students how to better understand language patterns and spelling strategies. Use them as lesson frames to be fine-tuned and built on. The activities vary in length and are presented as games to allow for greater instructional flexibility. There is not a sequential order to these activities, but there is a rationale for how they have been presented. Word Challenge is first because, as the core Pattern Activity, it should be used more frequently than the others. Prove the Pattern and Picking Out Patterns are listed next because they tend to be longer and more structured than the other tasks. Match the Meaning is listed last because the dictionary usage in this activity requires a higher level of reading comprehension than the other activities. All the remaining activities are comparable in regard to the time taken and their relative difficulty. Mix and match these Pattern Activities to best meet your instructional needs and time constraints. As you work with the activities, you will naturally gravitate to the ones that best fit your teaching style and classroom situation. Just keep in mind that for students to effectively learn a new skill, they need lots of opportunities to use it. The Pattern Activities are as follows:

Word Challenge

Prove the Pattern

Picking Out Patterns

Expanding Words

Chain Reaction

Scattered Syllables

Rhyme Time

Word Association

Word Detective

Match the Meaning

The Pattern Activities should be taught concurrently with the Thinking Activities because they help students to see the combined importance of sound, meaning, and visual information when spelling. Most other instructional approaches tend to emphasize visual memory in the middle grades. The result is that students are not consistently examining words deeply enough (Schlagal, 1992; Templeton, 1992a).

Sound and meaning patterns influence the spelling of many words. When we fail to consider such information, we ignore a number of helpful patterns that help words make better sense. Not surprisingly, students are more likely to generalize what they have learned when instruction explores the importance of sound, meaning, and visual information together (Westwood, 1999). Pattern and Thinking Activities attempt to better highlight the combined importance of these three types of information for students.

Choosing Words for Study

How you choose words for study can create barriers to in-depth study of words. Spelling words are often selected by their *frequency of use* at a grade level (Thomas, 1979). When this is the case, many related words (e.g., *real/reality/realistic/realization*) are taught separately from one another. Students are then not routinely making connections between words (Templeton, 1992a). By teaching related words together, you can take advantage of a wonderful teaching opportunity to demystify spelling–meaning connections for students. Keep this in mind as you choose word lists for the activities.

Starter Words for the Pattern Activities

Strategic Spelling teaches important patterns and spelling strategies rather than having students memorize high-frequency words; therefore, the words you select are less important than the conversations about words that you have with your class. Do not be overly concerned about finding the perfect words; they don't exist. Such a word list will never exist because the needs and abilities of students vary widely. In fact, with traditional spelling programs students may already know more than

50% of the words prior to beginning the program (Krashen, 1989; see also Curtiss & Dolch, 1939; Hughes, 1966; Thompson, 1930).

Lists of teacher-tested words are provided to get you started with the activities. Once you are comfortable with the activities, select words from such sources as the dictionary, classroom units, and other activities. One starter word can illustrate a variety of patterns, so it is not uncommon for a word in one activity to work well in another. The categories *are* somewhat arbitrary. When you come across a word for one activity that you think will work well in another activity, use it. Select words that you believe will be challenging and also teach some type of pattern.

Deepening the Study of Words

Teach students to deliberately consider sound, meaning, and visual information together. The best way to teach this is to combine traditionally isolated lessons, such as phonics, word attack skills, structural analysis, vocabulary, and spelling, into integrated lessons (Bear et al., 2000; Henderson & Templeton, 1986; Rosencrans, 1998; Tarasoff, 1990; Zutell, 1992).

Use the Word Challenge activity regularly—more than any other activity—to have students apply what they know about *all five* spelling strategies. (Note the comparative importance of the Word Challenge in Figure 1.) Incorporate other Pattern Activities into your instruction in a way that best meets the needs of your students. Use the Figure 1 rubric as a quick visual reference for choosing Pattern Activities that reinforce specific strategies.

The only spelling strategy not emphasized in the Pattern Activities is different spellings. This strategy is usually not difficult for students to grasp. To provide additional practice in this strategy, consider an instructional approach similar to that described in Homonym Headaches (see chapter 4).

Figure 1. Rubric of Patterning Activities and Spelling Strategies

	Rhyme	Syllables	Word-in-Word	Spelling–Meaning Connection	Different Spellings
Word Challenge	✓	✓	✓	✓	✓
Prove the Pattern	✓	✓	✓	✓	
Picking Out Patterns	✓	✓	✓		
Expanding Words	✓	✓	✓	✓	
Chain Reaction		✓	✓		
Scattered Syllables		✓	✓	✓	
Rhyme Time	✓	✓			
Word Association	✓	✓			
Word Detective		✓	✓	✓	
Match the Meaning			✓	✓	

Conclusion

The human brain is a pattern detector. We do not think about words by recalling and implementing complicated sequences of rules and exceptions. Accurate spelling occurs because our brains recognize familiar sounds, important letter combinations, and other predictable patterns. The following Pattern Activities reinforce natural pattern-detection tendencies. In the next chapter, the Thinking Activities help students overcome common spelling problems.

Word Challenge

Word Challenge is the core Pattern Activity because it consistently asks students to consider which spelling strategies work best, choose those strategies, then apply them with supporting evidence. By the middle grades, students are ready to learn to spell strategically. They are ready to think more deeply about how they are building words. This activity motivates them to apply strategies in order to spell challenging words. In addition, it complements the decoding students are doing in reading. Coltheart and Leahy (1996) suggest that in order to more easily use large letter combinations (e.g., *tion, ight, ough*), students need ample experience decoding unfamiliar words. The Word Challenge activity is an adjunct to the decoding process.

Materials

- photocopies of Reproducible 1, Spelling Strategies Diagram (one for each student)
- Reproducible 2, Word Lists for Word Challenge (select three to five words for each lesson)
- student notebooks
- dictionary

Advance Preparation

The words for the Word Challenge list can come from a variety of sources. To get started, refer to Reproducible 2. Other possible words can come from classroom units, the dictionary, a textbook, or lists your students create. Where the words came from, however, is not as important as making sure that they are predictable and challenging.

Select three to five words for the word list that are challenging and relatively unfamiliar to students (rather than words they can automatically recall). This activity should force students to more deliberately consider a wider range of sound, visual, and meaning patterns. Using difficult words also frees students from the expectation that they *should* be able to spell every word perfectly. It places greater emphasis on the thinking process that leads to accurate spelling. Using this approach, students' word accuracy is still measured, but so are

- gradual improvements in accuracy,
- appropriate strategy use, and
- whether they are noticing useful patterns.

Word Challenge's equal emphasis on strategy usage, evidence, and accurate spelling allows students to better see incremental signs of improvement. The linking of strategies and evidence helps students to see if they are using appropriate strategies and patterns.

Lesson Format

Time Required: Approximately 20–30 minutes for three to five words. Word presentation typically takes two-thirds of the lesson. During this time, students list the most logical spelling for each word, record the strategies they have used, and provide evidence of why their strategy works. Word analysis takes about one-third of the lesson. It involves examining the words with students and scoring the activity.

Objective: Students will create reasonably accurate word spellings from dictated challenge words. These predicted spellings will be supported by appropriate spelling strategies and evidence to show the logic behind their spelling.

Procedure:

1. Ask students to open their notebooks and set up a Word Challenge list, writing these

headings across the top row: Words, Strategies, and Evidence. (Figure 2 presents a sample Word Challenge list.)

2. Remind students that they can refer back to their Spelling Strategies Diagram at any time.

3. Dictate the first word to the class three or four times.

- Remind students that their evidence needs to show that their strategies work.

- Encourage students to list more than one strategy.

- To speed up written responses, teach abbreviations such as S/M/C for spelling–meaning connection, W/W for word-in-word, and D/S for different spellings.

4. While the students are working, model how to use the dictionary by looking up the word. Share the most common meaning as simply as possible, and remind students to think about spelling–meaning connections.

5. Dictate the word one or two more times to provide additional "think time" before moving on to the next word.

6. Repeat the first four steps for all the words in the list.

7. Once students have finished recording their answers, analyze the words as a class.

Consider this part of the lesson to be your instructional time. It is your opportunity to reinforce proper strategy usage and to push students to further examine the logic in their spelling. To maximize the effect of this marking process, note the following:

- Each student should mark his or her own work.

- Words should be marked and discussed one at a time.

- **Do not** immediately indicate which answer is correct. Instead, accept three or four possible spellings for each word, and list these spellings, strategies, and evidence on the board. This technique maximizes interest because you end up listing many of your students' individual spellings and strategies prior to the discussion.

- Remember to use abbreviations (e.g., S/M/C for spelling–meaning connection).

- Have your class vote on which spelling "looks right." This process encourages students to become more aware of their own spelling instincts and increases interest because everyone wants to see if their choice is correct.

- Use student examples to discuss what common patterns or strategies best helped to determine the correct spelling.

Figure 2. Sample Word Challenge List

Words	Strategies	Evidence
1. electrocardiograph	Syllables Word-in-Word	e·lec·tro·car·dio·graph electro, car, card, graph
2. incomprehensible	Syllables Spelling–Meaning Connection	in·com·pre·hens·i·ble comprehend
3. cream	Rhyme Different Spellings	scream stream, team, theme, beam

If the class agrees on a correct spelling, discuss what patterns might have led them to this common conclusion.

Reinforcing the Spelling Strategies

When analyzing and scoring words with your class, remember to reinforce the spelling strategies:

- Good spellers use a variety of strategies.

- Long and short vowels indicate where to break syllables.

- Words often break into syllables between double letters (e.g., *hel·lo, fun·ny*).

- Meaning affects the spelling of many multi-syllable words.

- The spelling of smaller words within larger ones often remains unchanged.

- The rhyming strategy is most effective with short words and endings of longer words.

- Only use the different spellings strategy with relatively familiar words.

Activity Scoring

The best way to score the Word Challenge list is to mark each word attempt out of a total of 3 possible points:

- 1 point for the correct spelling

- 1 point for using appropriate strategies

- 1 point for providing evidence to support the strategies used

This balanced scoring system allocates the majority of points to students' use of logic. Greater value is placed on students' thinking than on the final answer. To maximize student participation, consider the following:

- For long or challenging words, give half points if a student is within a letter of the correct spelling. (Half points acknowledge to students that some letter combinations are more difficult to decipher than others.)

- Only give full marks in the Strategies column if the student lists two or more appropriate strategies.

- Using positive feedback and random rewards, recognize students who achieve an exceptional score, provide particularly detailed evidence, or demonstrate above-average strategy usage. This takes very little time yet has a powerful positive influence on student attitude and motivation. Potential random rewards include a special privilege, positive written comments, candy, stickers, and bonus marks.

Teaching Tips

- To create more powerful discussions during scoring, select one or two words that have patterns from recent Thinking Activities (see chapter 4).

- To best motivate your students, frame this activity as a challenge. Such an approach can be very effective because, in essence, you are daring them to try to spell words they don't know. In my own classroom I regularly told students, "These words are high school and university words. You shouldn't really be able to spell them, but if you are smart and use your spelling strategies, you can probably figure many of them out."

- When students use the rhyme strategy, encourage them to list three or four examples to find the dominant pattern. If two patterns appear equally, remind students that the English language is not 100% predictable. Ask students which pattern looks and feels right. Most times they will know.

- Have students find challenging words to use in future lessons. This task generates a lot of critical thought if you insist that students also provide strategies and evidence to prove how someone else could logically deduce the correct spelling of their word. Publicly thank the individual students when using their words in the activity (they love it).

Special Needs Considerations

This activity is appropriate for most ELLs and students with learning challenges. Almost any student who can read and write independently can successfully complete this task at his or her own level of functioning. Even students who struggle with daily spelling enjoy this activity because of its clear structure, concrete strategy usage, and balanced scoring. They quickly learn which strategies to use and can provide good evidence, but their words are still often misspelled. They simply do not have a deep enough understanding of underlying language patterns to consistently spell some complex words accurately. For these students, I have found it helpful to emphasize the importance of the process and to highlight smaller successes:

- I remind them the most important part of this activity is that they are practicing the strategies good spellers use. Whether or not they manage to spell these very challenging words accurately is secondary.

- I positively reinforce proper use of strategies and evidence.

- I highlight accurate spelling patterns within words to show students that their spelling skills are improving.

When these simple strategies are used in conjunction with the Word Challenge balanced scoring system, even students with special needs experience success.

Extension: Wild Words Game Show

The Wild Words Game Show is a group extension of the Word Challenge activity. When presented in a game format, this task is a great way to get students talking and thinking together about how words are built. This team task follows the same basic process as the Word Challenge activity except students must agree on the word spellings, evidence, and strategies listed on their team papers. This format creates a great deal of group discussion. The extension procedure is as follows:

1. Create teams of two to three students.

2. Allow each team to come up with a name for their team.

3. Lay the team ground rules: Insist that *every* student must write equally on the team paper.

4. Start the activity with a catchy tune to set the tone as if it were a game show or contest. Students respond well to this activity when it is presented in this manner.

5. Follow the Word Challenge activity steps.

6. For best results mark the individual words with the groups as they complete them. List team scores on the board to increase student interest.

Prove the Pattern

Good spellers use a number of systematic spelling strategies (Gable et al., 1988; Gentry, 1982). Unfortunately, many students use only one strategy: sounding out. Prove the Pattern trains students to consider a range of spelling strategies. It reviews how to use several strategies to spell *one word* rather than spell several words using the same strategy. This explicit practice shows students how to better use their word knowledge, a skill that is essential if students are to become good spellers (Schlagal, 1992; Templeton, 1992a, 1992b; Westwood, 1999).

Materials

- photocopies of Reproducible 1, Spelling Strategies Diagram (one for each student)
- photocopies of Reproducible 3, Prove the Pattern (one for each student)
- one or two preselected root words
- dictionaries (one for each student)

Advance Preparation

Choose one or two words that you feel would be of interest to your class. They might be words connected to an upcoming unit or something related to a recent lesson. For best lesson results, ensure that chosen words contain predictable patterns and have a number of related words clustered around them in the dictionary. Some starter word examples follow:

approachability	*circumnavigation*
assemblage	*exhibition*
biodiversity	*hemispherical*
carbonization	*metallurgy*
cinematographer	*meteorologically*

Lesson Format

Time Required: Approximately 10 minutes per word (including discussion).

Objective: Students will use a range of spelling strategies to examine language patterns present within selected words.

Procedure:

1. Distribute the photocopies of Reproducible 1 and Reproducible 3.

2. Dictate the preselected root word three or four times for the class to write down on Reproducible 3 beside "1. Predicted spelling."

3. Ask students to complete numbers 2–5. These "tests" help students determine whether their predicted spelling makes logical sense.

4. Allow students to use their dictionaries to answer numbers 6 (words connected by meaning) and 7 (actual spelling).

5. If students experience difficulty before they get to 6, consider allowing them to use the dictionary sooner or allowing them to discuss with their neighbors what they have noticed.

6. When students have had sufficient time to complete the task, mark it either as a class or collect and mark individually. Regardless of the marking method chosen, remember that the time spent reviewing these answers with students is your instructional time. Ensure that you discuss patterns within words and connections between words when examining these answers with your students.

Reinforcing the Spelling Strategies

When analyzing and scoring words with your class, remember to reinforce the following:

- Good spellers use all of these strategies at one point or another.

- Long and short vowels indicate where to break syllables.

- Words often break into syllables between double letters (e.g., *hel·lo, fun·ny*).

- The rhyming strategy is most effective with short words and endings of longer words.

- The spelling of smaller words within larger ones often remains unchanged.

- Words with similar meanings have similar spellings and are often clustered together in the dictionary.

Activity Scoring

A 5-point marking scale that awards 1 point for each accurate "strategy" response works well in this activity. You can also award marks for the predicted spelling and actual spelling, but because the focus of this activity is on correct strategy usage, I have often limited my marking focus to the strategies only.

Teaching Tips

- This activity is most effective when limited to just two words per lesson.

- To ensure that all students remain productive, circulate and monitor progress. Announce at opportune moments the minimum point students are expected to have reached. This helps some students better manage their time.

Special Needs Considerations

Students with learning difficulties may sometimes initially struggle with this activity's multiple steps and dictionary usage. Once familiar with the process, however, most will complete the activity as successfully as any of their peers. For these students, check more frequently for understanding, and provide additional examples or assistance as needed.

Picking Out Patterns

This activity helps students become cognitively aware of *how* they spell by separating words based on important patterns within the word. Students slow down and consciously examine how letter patterns are put together to form a word. There is no lone letter pattern or strategy that students can rely on in all spelling situations. There are, however, many reliable letter patterns that students can use. To learn to spell well, students need to know how words work—how they go together (Zutell, 1992). This activity's flexible format allows teachers to decide which letter patterns are most important for their students to review at any given time. It provides another instructional opportunity to more explicitly link spelling strategies and letter patterns.

Materials

- photocopies of Reproducible 1, Spelling Strategies Diagram (one for each student)
- photocopies of Reproducible 4, Picking Out Patterns Table (one for each student)
- list of the three target spelling patterns
- list of words

Advance Preparation

Choose words for this activity from traditional spelling lists, content area textbooks, units being studied, or from starter words given for other activities. The number of words on the list will depend on the students' abilities and time available. Select the spelling patterns you want your students to find within the words they are studying. Some of these patterns, such as syllables or word-in-word, are highlighted within the actual spelling strategies. Other spelling patterns based upon sound, meaning, or visual cues can also provide students with important

insights into how words are built. Some good word patterns to study include

- double letters at syllable junctures
- letters dropped or added
- long/short vowel sounds (open or closed syllables)
- past, present, and future tenses
- phonetic sounds (e.g., /k/)
- prefixes, suffixes
- root words
- silent letters
- syllables
- words within a word

Lesson Format

Time Required: Approximately 30–40 minutes for 10 words.

Objective: Students will be able to identify important spelling patterns from the words listed and record these findings on the Picking Out Patterns Table.

Procedure:

1. Provide students with photocopies of Reproducible 1 and Reproducible 4.

2. Review the three word patterns you want students to focus on (e.g., root word, syllables, added or dropped letters).

3. Ask students to write the names of the three patterns as their headings at the top of the columns on Reproducible 4. (A filled-in example is available in Figure 3.)

4. Remind students that spelling strategies take advantage of language patterns. Draw their attention to the final column, Spelling Strategies, and ask them to write in the

strategies that could best help them to spell the word in the first column.

5. Provide the words to be studied. Let 'em loose!

6. Monitor student progress and, to encourage a productive pace, state minimum points that the group is expected to have reached at various points during the activity.

7. Upon completion of the activity, decide whether it will be marked in class or handed in.

Reinforcing the Spelling Strategies

This activity is a useful way to highlight common spelling difficulties within your classroom. Simply select words that present the area(s) of difficulty, and select headings that reinforce these patterns or strategies to detect them.

Activity Scoring

In this activity, you could mark each individual answer for accuracy, or you could provide a more global overall mark for student accuracy, effort, and detail on the task. This second method uses a 5-point scale in which 5/5 is exceptional, 4/5 is good, 3/5 is satisfactory, 2/5 is work that needs improvements, and 1/5 is work that is incomplete or below grade-level expectations. Remember with both of these methods to consider the activity's summarizing sentence in your evaluation.

Teaching Tips

• Some selected words may not possess all of the targeted word patterns highlighted in your headings. For example, even though one of your headings might focus on suffixes, all

Figure 3. Sample Picking Out Patterns Table

Word	Root Word	Syllables	Added or Dropped Letters	Spelling Strategies
different	differ	dif•fer•ent	none	word in word rhyming syllables
probably	probable	prob•ab•ly	dropped an e, added an ly	syllables different spellings

your selected words may not contain a suffix. In such cases, simply tell your students to write "none" in the appropriate box.

• The first couple of times you teach this activity, be directive and walk the class through the process using two or three concrete examples.

Special Needs Considerations

Some students who have special needs can find the number of headings and boxes within this activity initially overwhelming. To best support them until they feel more comfortable with the format, consider the following:

• Check more frequently for comprehension.

• Provide additional concrete examples on students' sheets for reference.

• Reduce the number of categories (or words) these students need to complete.

Expanding Words

The average adult has a vocabulary of about 70,000 words. To help organize and understand these words, people rely on a core vocabulary of about 5,000 words (Henderson & Templeton, 1986; Rosencrans, 1998). They extrapolate from these known words to help them spell less frequently used ones. Students need to actively examine how word parts combine with root words to form new words (Ganske, 2000; Templeton & Bear, 1992a). Expanding Words gives students this opportunity. Students come to understand how affixes combine with root words to create a variety of connected words (see Figure 4). This activity works best as a race in which students try to list as many words as possible within a specified time frame.

Materials

- preselected starter word
- timer
- student notebooks
- dictionaries (one for each student)

Advance Preparation

Choose words from a dictionary or other books in your classroom for this activity. The best ones tend to be short words or words with Latin or Greek roots. In both cases, these words or word roots need to be connected to many other related words. When choosing a word, scan the dictionary page to get a sense of how many other related words students will be able to find. This will give you a good initial sense of whether it is going to be a word students can successfully expand. Some starter words include the following:

coal	*ship*	*self*
over	*sub*	*treat*
sea	*super*	

Lesson Format

Time Required: Approximately 10 minutes per starter word (including discussion time).

Objective: Students will be able to apply what they know about affixes and spelling–meaning connections to generate a series of related words from a single starter word.

Procedure:

1. Write the starter word on the board.

2. Emphasize to students that all the words that will be listed on the board must be connected in *meaning* to the starter word. Then challenge students to brainstorm as many related words as possible.

3. Set a timer for five minutes per word in order to encourage the feeling of a race. Tell them that their job is to beat the clock by creating an expanded word list that includes more related words than your secret target number. To ensure maximum participation, do not share this secret number until after the activity is complete. This allows you to monitor student progress during the task and adjust your secret number accordingly. This method also allows for numerous students to experience success because you can have many students

Figure 4. Expanding Words Sample

act

activity	action	
acting	acted	
react	reacting	
reacted	activation	*You may find students will be able to produce well over 20 connected words.*
activate	activities	
activating	acting	
actor	reactionary	
reactor	react	

beat the clock instead of having only one game winner. For best results, limit this activity to one or two starter words per lesson.

4. Have students list their connected words below the starter word in their notebooks. Often students are able to brainstorm well over 20 words.

5. If students begin to struggle, remind them to consider prefixes and suffixes and to use their dictionaries because many words with similar meanings are often clustered closely together.

6. When the timer sounds, ask students to add up the total number of words they have listed.

7. To quickly determine who has beaten your secret target number, ask students to raise their hands if they have listed a specified number of words. Raise this number until you have reached your target number and congratulate those students whose hands remain.

8. Conclude this activity with a minilesson to reinforce an important language pattern (i.e., common affixes). I have often created an overhead copy of a student's expanded list (with permission) to review and discuss with the class.

9. Collect student assignments to mark for completion.

Reinforcing the Spelling Strategies

Discuss with students how the ongoing removal and addition of affixes and the frequent combining of small words allows students to better see how the spelling strategies of syllabication, word-in-word, and spelling–meaning connection contribute to the expansion of related words from a common root word.

Activity Scoring

In the past, I have often just collected students' brainstormed lists and marked them as complete or incomplete. The brainstorming nature of this activity makes it difficult to mark with a numerical value. Instead, try and treat this activity more as a game, and use students' completed lists as the basis for your instruction. If you wish to gather a numerical mark, consider using the 5-point scale discussed in the previous activity.

Teaching Tips

• To maximize participation, occasionally offer a reward for behaviors such as working well together, using dictionaries effectively, and being exceptionally focused. This type of reinforcement works particularly well with students who have learning difficulties, poor motivation, or limited confidence (Westwood, 1999). All students respond well to positive reinforcement that clearly indicates the behaviors you value.

• Until students become comfortable with this activity, consider accepting words that may not have a spelling–meaning connection (e.g., *coal* and *coalesce*). Once students are familiar with the process, more strictly enforce this spelling–meaning criteria.

• Consider using Latin or Greek roots as morning ice breakers or quick thinking activities to begin your spelling lessons. List one of these affixes on the board and challenge your students to figure out its underlying meaning. To make the task more concrete, encourage students to compare related words to this root. After they have independently examined the root's meaning, ask them to share with a neighbor. Tell them to pay close attention to their partner's answer because they will need to do something with this information. When students have finished sharing, discuss the root's meaning as a class. When the right answer has been determined, ask students to raise their hands or give a thumbs-up sign if their partner predicted the actual meaning during the sharing time. This quick comprehension check forces students to pay more attention to what their partners have said.

Special Needs Considerations

Most ELLs and students with learning difficulties are very successful with this activity because it can be easily done at their level of functioning. The most common difference between these students and their classmates is that their lists are not as lengthy. If a student is struggling to generate enough related words, consider a quick review of common prefixes (*un-*, *pre-*) and suffixes (*-s*, *-ed*, *-ing*). List these affixes on students' pages as a visual reference. Also, remind struggling students to use the dictionary because related words are often clustered together in the dictionary. Additional supports such as these help to structure this activity into smaller, more manageable steps.

Extension: Expanding Word Teams

To extend this activity into a cooperative task, simply divide the class into teams of two to four students and follow the lesson steps again. Still insist that *every* student create his or her own word list, but this time tell students that you will only select one student list from each team. This twist forces students to work together to ensure that every team member has a similar list because they don't know whose list will eventually be selected. Recognize teams who won in a manner that makes sense within the context of your classroom. It can be the team with the highest total or those teams who "beat the clock" by listing a specified number of words within the time provided. If you have any students in your class with significant written output issues, you may also want to consider quietly telling them and their group that you will not be selecting that student's notebook to represent the group score at the end of the activity. This adaptation prevents peers from putting unrealistic pressure on students who struggle to put pen to paper. Instead, write on top of these students' pages the number of words you expect them to finish.

Chain Reaction

There is a natural tendency for elementary school students to use frequently pronounceable word parts, such as syllables, small words inside bigger ones, and rhyme, as decoding strategies (Gunning, 1995; Hardy, Stennett, & Smythe, 1973; Henderson, 1990; Rubeck, 1977). Both Chain Reaction and Expanding Words reinforce this ability by getting students to build words. The difference between the two activities is their starting point. Expanding Words begins with a starter word to which students add affixes. In this activity, students begin with an affix to create a chain of new words, as shown:

-ment   government, pavement, resentment, movement, torment

ex-   exchange, exhale, exhaust, exhibit, exhume

in-   indefinite, increase, indentation, incorrect, individual

Chain Reaction works best as a game in which students race to beat the clock. The goal is for students to complete two or three chains of words as quickly as possible. This activity works well as an individual task, but it can be played in partners if you want greater interaction between students. The exact number of words students create in each chain will depend on how advanced your students are. Four to eight words per affix is not an unreasonable expectation for a middle school classroom.

Materials

- preselected affixes (three per lesson works well)
- student notebooks
- timer

Advance Preparation

From the following list, select three common affixes to be used by students to start their word chains:

Prefixes

dis-	mis-	sub-
ful-	non-	super-
in-	pre-	trans-
inter-	re-	

Suffixes

-able	-ful	-ise
-ance	-ion	-ment

The exact combination of prefixes and suffixes you choose depends on the needs of your students. Consider repeating certain troublesome affixes so that students have repeated opportunities to review these problem patterns.

Lesson Format

Time Required: Approximately 15 minutes to complete and discuss three word chains (including student marking).

Objective: Students will be able to quickly brainstorm a number of words that are connected by common affixes.

Procedure:

1. Have students set up their notebooks for the activity and hand out dictionaries.

2. Describe how Chain Reaction is played (see introduction), and tell students how many words should be included in each chain.

3. Explain how many words need to be in each affix chain, and remind students that they

cannot move on to subsequent chains until the one they are working on is finished.

4. To ensure your students are actively thinking about the words, remind them that to successfully beat the clock they need to have accurate spellings and know the meanings of their words.

5. List your chosen affixes on the board and start your timer.

6. When the timer sounds, ask students to take a minute to review their lists to ensure their words are spelled correctly and that they know what each one means.

7. Ask students to exchange books with a neighbor. Tell them that for this part of the activity, they get to be the teacher and mark their partner's word chains for accuracy. Direct them to place a small check mark above the words that are spelled correctly. Encourage students to use dictionaries. Once they have finished marking, ask them to choose two words and quiz their partner on the meanings of these words. If the partner cannot provide a reasonable definition for the word, then it is not correct. Tell students to total up the number correct and return the notebook.

8. Ask students who beat the clock by accurately finishing the affix word chains within the allotted time frame to raise their hands. Congratulate these students and choose one or two of these notebooks to use as examples. List a few words from these notebooks on the board to discuss.

9. Collect the notebooks for marking (optional).

Reinforcing the Spelling Strategies

When reviewing your students' sample words, reinforce how spelling strategies such as syllabication, word-in-word, rhyming, different spellings, and spelling–meaning connections can aid in spelling accuracy. In these conversations, make part of your instructional focus about affixes and spelling–meaning connections. When prefixes and suffixes are attached to a word, they change the meaning of that word; for example, the prefix *pre-* means *before*, the suffix *-ed* changes a verb to past tense, and *-ing* indicates the present. Highlight these spelling–meaning connections by removing affixes and discuss changes in word meaning.

Activity Scoring

I tend to mark this activity with the students during class time using the process described in the Lesson Format section. I follow this up by collecting student notebooks at the end of the lesson and simply placing a check mark at the bottom of the assignment to indicate that it is complete. If you wish to assign a numerical value to this activity, consider assigning a point for every correct word or using the 5-point scale discussed in the Picking Out Patterns activity.

Teaching Tips

- Provide students with regular feedback about how much time remains for them to beat the clock. This regular feedback improves student focus and participation.

- Frame this activity more as a game with a brief minilesson afterward. This philosophy helps to keep the tone of the activity fun and motivating for students.

- Summarizing dictionary definitions is a difficult task for many students in the middle grades. Consider asking students to find in the dictionary and summarize in their own words some of the words from these affix chains. Be sure to ask for a dictionary page number to ensure that they actually look up the word.

Special Needs Considerations

Most ELLs and students with learning difficulties are successful with this activity because it can be easily done at their level of functioning. The most common adaptation is to reduce the number of chains these students complete. If a student is struggling to generate enough related words, remind him or her to also use the dictionary for help. For extremely low-level students, use only prefixes as word chain starters because these are easier to locate in a dictionary.

Scattered Syllables

When competent writers spell, they do not refer to a set of rules to remember word patterns; instead they think of known letter patterns (Stahl, 1992). Some letter combinations never go together; others are almost never separated. Several letter combinations are used primarily at the end of a word (e.g., *-dge* and *-tion*). Others, such as *mis-* and *pre-*, are used at the start of a word. Scattered Syllables reinforces the recognition and use of predictable letter patterns such as these by asking students to decipher words that have been scrambled and divided into syllable parts. This activity can be a fun beginning or ending to any lesson.

Materials

• Reproducible 5, Starter Words for Scattered Syllables

• student notebooks

Advance Preparation

Use the starter words provided in Reproducible 5 the first few times you lead the activity. Once students are comfortable with the activity, use words that are more relevant to current content areas. Write the words on the board or prepare an overhead of the scrambled words.

Lesson Format

Time Required: Variable depending on the number of words selected. A range of 5 to 10 words often works well. Plan for about 3 minutes per word. This estimate includes student completion time and follow-up review.

Objective: Students will apply what they know about syllabication and letter patterns to reorganize scrambled words back into a readable format.

Procedure:

1. Have students set up notebooks for the activity.

2. Present the scrambled words. The first few times you do the activity, use fairly common words (and affixes) and keep the order of the individual syllables, as shown:

   publication   ubp/il/ac/noti
   (mix letters, retain syllable order)

3. Monitor your class to ensure students are on task and so you know when the majority of students are finished.

4. Review each of the scrambled words with the class. When marking, highlight important patterns such as those listed within the next section.

5. Collect marked work, or ask students to return notebooks to the rightful owner.

Reinforcing the Spelling Strategies

Look for opportunities to review important patterns:

• Certain letter patterns regularly go together.

• Location within a word can influence what letters are used.

• Vowel sounds can influence where syllable breaks go.

• Syllable breaks often split two of the same letter (e.g., *syl·la·ble*).

Activity Scoring

Assign one mark for each correctly unscrambled word.

Teaching Tips

• Remind students about the important syllable patterns:

  ○ Every syllable needs a vowel.

  ○ If it is a short vowel it will probably be sandwiched in the middle of the syllable between two consonants (e.g., *spel·ling*); if it is a long vowel it will likely be at the end of the syllable (e.g., *la·zy*).

  ○ Syllable breaks often split double letters (e.g., *fol·low*, *man·ner*).

• As students become comfortable with the process, make the activity more challenging by scrambling both the individual letters and the syllables (so that they are not in order):

  illustrative   li/slu/tar/veit
  (mix letters, retain syllable order)

  dealership   re/phsi/elad
  (mix letter and syllable order)

• If you ask students to mark their classmates' work, require them to always write their name in the bottom right-hand corner of the page. This simple step heightens student accountability to do a good job because it is always clear who marked the work.

Special Needs Considerations

Some students with special needs find having all the letters in these words scrambled overwhelming. If this situation occurs, consider deciphering the first and possibly even the last syllable to give them some concrete starting points. Also consider reducing the number of words if students have a slow work rate.

Rhyme Time

This activity is framed as a game during which students are asked to brainstorm related rhyming words. It is an important concept to practice because we naturally divide syllables into two parts: The *onset* describes letters before the vowel, and the *rime* includes the vowel and what comes after (Trieman, 1985). This division means that we naturally separate a word such as *man* into *m* (onset)/*an* (rime). This activity and Word Association that follows help to further reinforce patterns of syllabication and rhyme that students need when decoding multisyllable words. This activity can also be used with younger students operating in the Within Word Pattern developmental stage because of the type of skills it reinforces.

Materials

• Reproducible 6, Starter Words for Rhyme Time and Word Association

• student notebooks

• timer

Advance Preparation

Decide how your teams will be determined. Will student groupings be selected randomly, or do you have particular student combinations you wish to see? Preselect the rhyming words you wish to use from the starter words provided in Reproducible 6.

Lesson Format

Time Required: Variable depending on the number of words selected. A game can continue for a set time limit or for a set number of words. A game consisting of approximately 10 to 12 words often works well. Plan for about 2 to 3 minutes per word. This estimate includes student completion time and follow-up review.

Objective: Students will be able to quickly brainstorm a list of related rhyming words and then select from this list the least common one.

Procedure:

1. Divide class into teams of approximately four students.

2. Have students set up their notebooks for the activity.

3. Remind students that to score points in this game, they must write down a rhyming word that is different from those chosen by all the other students in their group, one that has not been duplicated by someone else.

4. Read aloud the list of words for students to rhyme one word at a time (provide adequate think time). A typical Rhyme Time game proceeds in this manner:

Teacher: "Your first rhyming word is *kite*. Choose an original word to rhyme with *kite*. One that you think no other person in your group will write down. *Kite*." (Wait 30–60 seconds.)

Students: Discuss in groups what rhyming words were chosen and mark accordingly. (See Activity Scoring.)

Repeat this process for the remaining words.

5. When all the words have been read, ask students to compare their rhyming words with those of the other students in the group. Any student who has listed a word that was not duplicated receives a point. Ask students to total up scores to determine winner(s).

6. Choose a couple of words listed by students and discuss.

Reinforcing the Spelling Strategies

Although this activity is primarily a rhyming task, it can also be used to reinforce other spelling strategies as well. After the words have been compared and marked within the student groups, examine a few of them as a class. With shorter words, ask students to expand the word into other related words by adding prefixes, suffixes, or combining with other words to create a compound word. When using longer multisyllable words, examine other patterns and/or spelling strategies such as root words, syllables, affixes, words within words, and spelling–meaning connections.

Activity Scoring

The easiest method to mark this activity is to verbally review student answers. If a student has a word that has not been duplicated, tell them to place a "✓" beside it. If student has listed a word that someone else in the group has duplicated, they place an "x" beside it. The winning player(s) have the most checks at the end of the game.

Teaching Tips

- Once students are comfortable with this game, raise the difficulty by creating increasingly larger groups and by asking them to rhyme the ends of longer multisyllable words.

- Play this game for a couple of rounds. After the first game, reshuffle your groups so that students play others who are more or less their own ability level (e.g., place group winners together). Another variation is to play this game in teams of two or three students. This format significantly increases discussion because students need to agree upon which unique word they will write down upon their group's answer sheet.

Special Needs Considerations

Most ELLs and students with special needs enjoy this game because they can easily complete it at their level of functioning. Unfortunately, some may not find unique rhyming words as quickly as their peers. To compensate for this, organize the groupings so that these students are sometimes grouped with peers of comparable ability. These students also benefit from instruction to remind them that a good method to find related rhyming words is to systematically replace the initial letter with others. For example, if they need to rhyme a word with *mop*, they can drop the *m* and insert other letters in its place to create words such as *bop, cop, drop, flop, hop, pop,* and *top*.

Word Association

Word Association follows a process similar to Rhyme Time except students try to brainstorm as many rhyming words as possible within a specified time frame. This activity can also easily be used with younger students operating in the Within Word Pattern developmental stage. There are many variations to this game, but it seems to work best when presented as a beat-the-clock race. Words can be presented by the teacher or by partners, and answers can be oral or written down. This quick and engaging activity works well at the beginning or end of any lesson. To help you get started, some of the most frequent rimes (refer to Gunning, 1995) have been provided in Reproducible 6.

Materials

- Reproducible 6, Starter Words for Rhyme Time and Word Association

- student notebooks (optional)

- timer

Advance Preparation

Decide whether students will complete this activity individually or with partners. If they will be working with partners, do you have particular student combinations in mind? Preselect the words you wish to use from the starter words provided in Reproducible 6. If students play with partners, remember that you will need a separate list of words for each student.

Lesson Format

Time Required: Variable depending on the number of words selected. A game consisting of approximately 7 words per partner (14 total) will take about 15 minutes when students complete written responses. Five to 10 minutes are required when students use verbal responses. This estimate includes student completion time and follow-up review.

Objective: Students will be able to quickly brainstorm lists of related rhyming words from a series of starter words.

Procedure:

1. Divide the class into partners if playing game with verbal responses. Partners are not necessary if students are writing the words they brainstorm.

2. Have students set up their notebooks if they are completing written answers.

3. The teacher or student partners slowly read out the list of starter words for students to brainstorm. If answers are verbal, use a time frame of 15–20 seconds per word. If answers are written, use a time frame of 45–60 seconds.

4. If playing this game verbally, make sure students know signals such as "pass" or "change" to help them move quickly from one word to another. A typical Word Association game being played verbally with partners proceeds in this manner:

   Student 1: *cap*

   Student 2 (verbal or written): *flap, wrap, strap, map, tap,*...change

   Student 1: *sit*

   Student 2 (verbal or written): *bit, lit, fit, wit, knit,*...change

   Repeat this process for the remaining words.

5. When students play with partners, ensure that both students have had an opportunity to brainstorm. Then ask students to total up how many words they listed.

6. Take a moment to discuss with students how a few of the rhyming words might be expanded into related words by adding affixes or other words. See Reinforcing the Spelling Strategies for more details.

Reinforcing the Spelling Strategies

Although this activity is primarily a rhyming task, it can also be used to reinforce other strategies. After students finish brainstorming their lists of related words, examine a few as a class. Ask students to expand some of these words into other related words by adding prefixes or suffixes or by combining with other words to create compound words. Tell them to create a number of words that have a spelling–meaning connection with the word being discussed.

Activity Scoring

For scoring purposes, insist that the words students generate are real. Partners can easily count how many rhyming words their classmate finds by using check marks or tallies. If students are writing down related rhyming words, have them count up the number they have listed. If you wish to assign a numerical value to this activity, complete it as an individual written task (not verbally in partners). Use a 5-point scale to indicate the quality of work. Provide students with criteria for how many words they must generate to attain a certain score (e.g., 30 related words must be listed to attain 5/5).

Teaching Tips

- To maximize student interest, consider playing this game using the secret number strategy outlined in the Expanding Words activity. This format allows many students to feel that they have been successful rather than only having one winner.

- Reduce preparation time by creating just one list and place it on an overhead projector (uncover words as needed). When students play with partners, position students brainstorming related words with their backs to the overhead projector, and face those providing the words toward it.

Special Needs Considerations

ELLs and students who have special needs often enjoy this game because they can complete it at their level of functioning. Special considerations for this activity are very similar to those listed within Rhyme Time. Remember to review how to find related rhyming words by systematically replacing a word's initial letter with other letters. If students have written output or cognitive processing speed issues, also consider adapting the criteria for success so that these students need to brainstorm fewer words to be successful.

Word Detective

The meanings of many multisyllable words can be pieced together by considering the meanings of smaller words or affixes within them. Our students need more opportunities to consider how spelling and meaning are connected. From the fifth grade on, students encounter about 10,000 new words every year (Nagy & Anderson, 1984). Most of these words are long, content-specific words that students must decipher in order to understand the reading (Cunningham, 1998). Word Detective helps students better understand why words are built in specific ways.

Materials

- Reproducible 7, Starter Words for Word Detective (select three to five starter words)
- student notebooks
- dictionaries (one for each student)
- thesauruses for each student (optional)

Advance Preparation

Use the sample words provided in Reproducible 7 or select your own words. Choose words that you feel would be of interest to your class. They might be words connected to an upcoming unit or related to a recent lesson. Consider beginning with compound words because they blend two words with distinct meanings into a new word that carries the meaning of both.

Lesson Format

Time Required: Approximately 5 minutes per starter word.

Objective: Students will be able to create a logical word definition for a challenging starter word by examining word-in-word and synonym evidence.

Procedure:

1. Have students set up their notebooks using the following four headings: Word, Word-in-Word Evidence, Synonyms, My Definition. They will need repeat these headings for each word they examine. (Refer to Figure 5 for Word Detective samples.)

2. Write the first starter word on the board and ask students to copy it into their notebooks beside the Word heading.

3. Ask students to list all of the smaller words that are within the given word beside their Word-in-Word Evidence heading. Encourage students to treat prefixes and suffixes as words here because affixes possess their own distinct meanings and can affect the meaning of the word as a whole. If students are not sure what a particular prefix or suffix means, refer them to the dictionary.

4. Ask students to examine these smaller words and list the synonyms of any that significantly influence the meaning of the word beside their Synonyms heading. Remind students that a synonym is a word that has a similar meaning to the given word but is spelled differently. Explain that the meanings of the smaller words influence the meaning of the multisyllable words. By looking at the meanings of the words within the multisyllable word, students should be able to decipher the multisyllable word's meaning.

5. Ask students to use this information to write their own definition beside the My Definition heading. Emphasize that you are not interested in a dictionary definition but in *their* definitions. Students' definitions

should be based on the information they have collected within the previous two steps.

6. Once students have completed the task, either mark as a class or collect to mark them yourself and review at a later date. Remember, these discussions are your teaching time.

Reinforcing the Spelling Strategies

Regularly remind students about the importance of the spelling–meaning connections within the word(s) they are examining. Encourage them to look for clues in all parts of the starter word. This activity encourages students to use analogy and to compare the word or parts of the word to other words with similar meanings and spellings. Highlight these connections with students during the lesson and when marking.

Activity Scoring

Even though the examples in Figure 5 are not technically correct, I would mark them correct because they show good reasoning ability. To encourage students to think more deeply about their definitions, scoring would be as follows:

Word-in-Word Evidence: 1 point

Synonyms: 1 point

My Definition: 2 points

Total possible score: 4 points

Teaching Tips

- Many students benefit from completing some examples together as a class before completing this task independently.

Figure 5. Word Detective Samples

Example 1
1. Word: supertanker
2. Word-in-Word Evidence: super, tank, tanker
3. Synonyms:
   super = big, great
   tank = a container
4. My Definition: It is some type of big container.

Example 2
1. Word: antivaccinationism
2. Word-in-Word Evidence: anti, vaccine, tion, ism
3. Synonyms:
   anti = against
   vaccination = medicine, needle
4. My Definition: Someone who is against vaccinations.

- This lesson works well at the beginning or end of any lesson. It also provides an opportunity to teach students how to use a thesaurus. To ensure that students actually look up the synonyms in the thesaurus, insist that they include the thesaurus page numbers beside the synonyms they write.

- Limit this activity to a maximum of two or three words per session to maintain student interest.

Special Needs Considerations

Some students with special needs may have a little more difficulty with this activity because, in order to develop reasonable word definitions, they need to segment, analyze, and synthesize word information. Consider pairing any weaker students with more capable buddies and provide more frequent teacher support until they are comfortable with the process.

Match the Meaning

Match the Meaning is the final Pattern Activity because it is the most difficult one. This activity—as well as its extension, Quick Draw—helps students to see how word meanings emerge from the combination of a root, prefixes, and suffixes. It reinforces for students that words with similar meanings often have similar spellings. When students notice this connection, they are better able to understand why many words are not spelled the way they sound. Proficient spellers use the spelling–meaning connection strategy a great deal, yet many students—even in high school—remain unaware of it (Marsh, Friedman, Welch, & Desberg, 1980; Templeton, 1992a).

Materials

• photocopies of Reproducible 8, Match the Meaning Worksheet (one for each student)

• one or two preselected words

• dictionaries (one for each student)

Advance Preparation

To get started use the sample words that follow or other words that start with common prefixes, including *un-*, *dis-*, and *re-*. When you begin to preselect your own words, look for starter words that have spelling–meaning connections with many other words in the dictionary. By providing a number of related words, you make it easier for students to select a second word that they can more easily make sense of.

dictionary	*miner*	*solarium*
governance	*multiple*	*subterranean*
magnetosphere	*prejudice*	*terrorization*

Lesson Format

Time Required: Approximately 10 minutes for each word.

Objective: Students will examine dictionary definitions for two related words in order to explain how these words are both the same and different.

Procedure:

1. Write the beginning word on the board for students to copy to Reproducible 8.

2. Ask students to use the dictionary to find a second word that has a similar spelling and meaning and to write it in beside number 2 on the worksheet.

3. Ask students to read to themselves the dictionary definition of both words to determine how they are same and different, then have them answer numbers 3 and 4. (Figure 6 provides a completed example.)

4. Once the worksheet has been completed, either mark it as a class or collect to mark worksheets yourself and review at a later date. Remember, these discussions are your teaching time.

Reinforcing the Spelling Strategies

This activity reinforces spelling–meaning connections and helps students begin to distinguish subtle differences between related dictionary definitions. It is as much about reading comprehension as it is about spelling strategies. After your students have finished comparing their two words on the Match the Meaning Worksheet, select a couple of the more common examples and discuss. Examine what makes the words the same or different. Also highlight other obvious patterns such as syllabication, rhyming, and smaller words within the larger one.

Scoring the Activity

Mark this activity out of 5. Assign 1 point for basics such as name, date, and listing the beginning and connected words. Then assign 2 points for each of the next two sections. Tell students that a big part of their mark in these last two sections will be for how clearly they can explain the similarities and differences between their two words. Encourage them to slow down and include sufficient detail. In these last two sections, assign partial marks for students who have provided partial answers.

Teaching Tips

This compare-and-contrast task is difficult for some students because of the reading comprehension level required to interpret a dictionary definition. Depending on the abilities of your students, you may need to complete this activity in groups or in pairs until students have a good grasp of the process.

Special Needs Considerations

This compare-and-contrast task is difficult for ELLs and many students with special needs because of the reading comprehension level required. To minimize these reading comprehension difficulties, consider the following:

- Partner weaker students with stronger buddies.

- Provide more frequent and more direct individualized instruction with regard to what the dictionary definitions say. Discuss with these students the key words within the definitions.

- If staffing permits, have students select, preread, and discuss the words they will examine prior to the lesson.

- Complete this task as a small-group activity for students who really struggle with the reading demands of this activity. Stronger readers should still be expected to complete the task individually.

Figure 6. Sample Match the Meaning Worksheet

Match the Meaning

1. Beginning Word _____
   Sandstone
   _____

2. Connected Word_____
   Sandstorm
   _____

3. How are their meanings the same?
   The words are the same
   _____
   because both involve sand.
   _____
   _____
   _____
   _____

4. How are their meanings slightly different?
   They are different because
   _____
   sandstone is rock made of
   _____
   sand and sandstorm is
   _____
   talking about clouds of
   _____
   sand in a windstorm.
   _____

Extension: Quick Draw

To provide students with additional dictionary practice, consider presenting this activity as a game in which student teams race to beat the clock or against one another. Simply divide the class into teams of three or four students, hand out dictionaries, and ask everyone to place their hands on their desks to show they are ready. Then, dictate the beginning word for students to find in the dictionary. Stop the race when a number of students have raised their hands. Ask the first student(s) finished for the dictionary page number and wait for the remainder of the class to find the page and definition. Next, dictate a second related word for students to find, but do not make it a race because the second word is often in close proximity to the first. Ask the student teams to compare their two words and list in their notebooks, or on the Match the Meaning Worksheet, how they are the same and different. Discuss as a class what an acceptable answer would include. In this game format, assign points to teams whose team members are the first to find the original dictionary word and to those teams that can generate a reasonably accurate explanation of the similarities and differences between the two words. To keep student interest high, limit games to three or four pairs of words.

Thinking Activities

ffective teaching involves more than just telling. Students can better understand and apply language patterns when they learn them through a discovery process (Snowball, 1996). The Thinking Activities provide an alternative to traditional independent seatwork. In these activities, students work together to discover common patterns rather than just being told.

Five Target Spelling Patterns

By the middle grades, most students are competent readers and writers. They have progressed to the point where they can identify, analyze, and discuss important language patterns. In the Thinking Activities, students work through a series of tasks that help them notice language patterns that they would probably not notice on their own. The five patterns that research (Bear et al., 2000; Ganske, 2000; Kosnik, 1998) has indicated are important for students in the middle grades are as follows:

1. phonetic
2. vowel
3. consonant
4. syllabication
5. affix

Each Thinking Activity addresses one or more of these five target patterns.

Phonetic patterns are examined because sounding words out is the first strategy most students consider when attempting to spell a new word. A good knowledge of phonetic patterns allows students to begin to formulate spellings. This initial phonetic information, however, must be considered along with other visual and meaning information to consistently spell longer multisyllable words accurately.

The related study of vowel sounds has been incorporated because students in the middle grades need this knowledge to help them more consistently add or drop letters within multisyllable words (e.g., silent *e*). The spelling of many multisyllable words is influenced by whether the word contains short or long vowel sounds. Consonant letter patterns demonstrate the importance of vowel sounds (e.g., when adding a suffix to *can*, the *n* must be doubled to preserve the short /a/ vowel sound).

There are numerous reliable consonant patterns that students can use to spell more accurately. These consonant letter patterns can be influenced by a variety of factors. Some consonants are influenced by the letter immediately preceding or following them. For example, a /k/ sound is often spelled with a *ck* if it is preceded by a vowel (e.g., *clock*). Conversely, if it is preceded by another consonant, it is often spelled with only a *k* (e.g., *tank*). Many other consonants are influenced by their position within a word—*ph* makes the /f/ sound at the beginning of words, whereas *gh* makes this same sound primarily at the end of words. In many words, the consonant (or vowel) used is also influenced by spelling–meaning connections (e.g., in the word *criticize*, a *c* is used to make the /s/ sound rather than the letter *s* because of its spelling–meaning connection to *critic*). We need to have more discussion with our students to highlight these predictable letter patterns and to point out spelling strategies that can help them to spell more accurately.

Syllabication is also crucial for older students to practice because the syllable is the main perceptual unit when reading and writing. It is what students rely on when breaking multisyllable words into more manageable chunks. The study of syllabication can help students to know if a letter should be twinned, if another vowel is needed, and where a syllable break should be. Understanding how syllables work helps students to better combine words, roots, and affixes. It provides a foundation to help students understand that words related in meaning are often related in spelling as well (e.g., *fish* and *fishtail*, *ship* and *shipbuilder*).

The related study of affixes is crucial for helping older students further understand how words are built. These predictable letter combinations consistently affect the meaning and spelling of multisyllable words. Many spelling mistakes in the middle grades occur when prefixes and suffixes are being added. These patterns need to be more explicitly examined with students. Students need practice segmenting and recombining words with affixes to better notice when to double or drop letters. The endings of many words can also provide hints about which affix should be used. For example, when adding the suffixes *-able* and *-ible*, there is a very reliable pattern students can use. If a root word can be read as a stand-alone word, students should add the suffix *-able* (e.g., *understand* + *able*); if students do not recognize the root as a word, they should use *-ible* (e.g., *poss* + *ible*).

No lone strategy or pattern is enough to make someone a good speller. To emphasize the predictability within the English language, we need to teach all five of these target patterns as predictable and integrated parts a total language system.

Organization of the Thinking Activities

The Thinking Activities in this chapter attempt to target the language patterns that will be most useful for students in the middle grades. They are in order of complexity and are presented in three sections: (1) vowel patterns; (2) homonyms, syllabication, and affixes; and (3) spelling–meaning connections and peculiar plurals. These sections should be considered areas of focus and not rigid categories to be studied in isolation.

The first set of Thinking Activities reviews important vowel patterns that students learn in the primary years. This review of phonetic patterns provides students with significant insight into why words are built in certain ways. The activities are as follows:

How Short and Long Get Along

The Magic *e*

Create a Language

When Two Vowels Go Walking

Sneaky Sounds

Is It *ei* or *ie*?

Vowel Variations

Fat or Skinny CaKe?

Crack the Code

The second set of Thinking Activities, focused on homonyms, syllabication, and affixes, emphasizes adding and dropping letters:

Homonym Headaches

Ch, tch, cha!

Predictable Patterns

Prefixes and Suffixes Poster

Y Endings Are Easy

The Vanishing *e*

Become an Etymologist

ing Endings

Spelling Variations

The final Thinking Activities place more emphasis on derivational relationships involving spelling–meaning connections and peculiar plurals:

You're the Judge

Linking Letters

Y Do I Always Get Dropped?

When *f* Multiplies

Plurals: *s* or *es*?

Patterns Everywhere

Hidden Connections

ed Endings

All the activities emphasize thinking skills (including comparing, sorting, classifying, and summarizing) because research indicates that thinking-skills tasks are more effective instructional methods than memorization of rules and words (Bear et al., 2000; Morris, 1982). By helping students to discover important language patterns, you are teaching them to think about words as predictable puzzles that can be broken down and solved rather than memorized. Your role as the teacher, then, is to spend time responding to what students have discovered instead of telling them what to notice.

Questioning Techniques That Enhance Thinking Activities

The success or failure of a lesson can be significantly influenced by the tone it is delivered in. The more teachers use higher order thinking questions, the more students learn (Askew & Wiliam, 1995; Raths, Wasserman, Jonas, & Rothstein, 1986). In this methodology, the teacher encourages higher levels of thinking by questioning students in ways that require them to change or manipulate information.

Skillful questioning includes ample wait time. Often the time between when a teacher asks for a response and actually selects a student is less than two seconds. Research indicates that this time frame is not long enough (Askew & Wiliam, 1995; Raths et al., 1986). When questions are asked this quickly, many students become disengaged simply because they cannot process the information quickly enough to keep up.

You can further enhance student learning during the Thinking Activities by incorporating teaching-for-thinking questioning strategies (Raths et al., 1986) (see Figure 7). With these questioning techniques, you can extend student thinking by structuring your responses in ways that encourage student thinking. Sometimes teachers inadvertently limit student thinking by sharing their opinions. This tendency can create discussions that more closely resemble a game of guess the "correct" answer rather than a thoughtful examination of an issue.

Through the Thinking Activities, students notice many language patterns. Every activity highlights one target pattern, but the targeted pattern is not the only acceptable answer.

Figure 7. Teacher Responses That Encourage or Limit Thinking

Encourage student thinking by
- asking for student observations (e.g., "What did you notice?");
- repeating student statements so that students can consider them further;
- paraphrasing the main ideas of what students say; and
- asking for more information, including details, examples, comparisons, and predictions (e.g., "Tell me a bit more.").

Avoid limiting student thinking by
- agreeing or disagreeing with what students say (e.g., "Good answer!");
- failing to allow adequate wait time or cutting off students as they are responding;
- leading students to the "right" answer; and
- talking so much that students don't have a chance to respond.

Students will notice many interesting language patterns, so be careful not to discount their discoveries. As they start to take note of connected language patterns, discuss the patterns and their exceptions. Doing so will further heighten student awareness about the many visual, meaning, and sound patterns that they can use to spell better (Ganske, 2000). Teaching in this way conveys the message that you are exploring language patterns together to better understand how all words work. If you ignore students' spontaneous discoveries and focus immediately on the targeted word pattern, you risk limiting students' interest and thinking. No doubt many of the responses that encourage student thinking in Figure 7 are already part of your teaching repertoire.

Any way you respond to a student influences the classroom discussion. Try to maintain a balance between flexible thinking and discussion time, and time that emphasizes the activity's target pattern. Most often, students discover target patterns on their own because the patterns are the dominant ones present in the activity, but sometimes it may be necessary to subtly move the class toward the discovery of the targeted pattern. To do this, use nonjudgmental responses such as "thank you" to limit discussions from going too far astray. Conversely, when a student brings up an important point, extend the line of thinking by using responses that encourage further thought (e.g., "Tell me more."). Together, these two kinds of responses allow you to foster productive class discussions.

General Design of the Thinking Activities

The Thinking Activities follow a similar instructional design to the Pattern Activities. Most of the Thinking Activities use similar routines and strategies and follow a basic lesson format. The common features of the Thinking Activities are detailed here. Information specific to an activity is included with the activity text.

The Thinking Activities all follow a basic three-step process in which students brainstorm, examine, and explain what they discover. This type of "discovery learning" is a far more powerful way for students to learn than just being told the spelling rules (Caine & Caine, 1997; Raths et al., 1986; Snowball, 1996).

Each Thinking Activity first asks students to brainstorm a list of words to work with. Using words students know allows them to fully concentrate on finding the visual, sound, and meaning patterns (Henderson & Templeton, 1986; Templeton & Bear, 1992a; Zutell, 1992). Starter words are provided for those activities that students have had difficulty brainstorming enough suitable examples for, but try to maintain the focus on words students already know.

After the brainstorm, students are asked to perform a task that requires higher order thinking (e.g., interpreting, categorizing, or summarizing). The task draws out language patterns for students to examine. The activity then asks students to apply or explain the language pattern.

These Thinking Activities can be completed as individual assignments, but they work best when completed in cooperative groups of two or three students. When students have trouble learning something, they naturally turn to others for help. In middle-grade classrooms this often means that students turn to peers for assistance. This social process is one that we need to better exploit. By using small cooperative groups, you can help students at all levels develop a better understanding of words.

Materials

Most of the Thinking Activities require a reproducible and notebooks for students to complete their assigned work. The specific reproducible and other materials required are specified for each activity.

Advance Preparation

For each activity, advance preparation consists of photocopying a reproducible and previewing the lesson to ensure a clear understanding of the lesson's objective, format, and target spelling pattern. Any additional preparation has been noted in the individual activities.

Lesson Format

Time Required: The majority of these activities take approximately 30 minutes to complete. Different time requirements are noted where applicable.

Objective: Students will be able to brainstorm a set of appropriate sample words, examine these words for important language patterns, and summarize what patterns they notice.

Procedure: You can follow a basic set of procedures for most of the Thinking Activities. These procedures are not meant to be a rigid set of rules but rather a framework to be adapted and built on—use the instructional methods and sequence that best suit the needs of your class. Most of these Thinking Activities use what is known as a closed sort—the categories are predetermined. This structure allows for a guided discovery in which students deduce the understandings themselves rather than being directly taught. The closed structure also ensures that the tasks are limited enough in scope to be manageable for most students. A few of the word sorts are open—students generate their own categories based on word meanings, letter combinations, sounds, and other patterns. In these activities more instructional emphasis is placed on thinking rather than on conclusions. If an activity requires procedures that differ from the basic instructional framework described below, then this information has been provided within the individual activities.

1. Randomly divide the class into small teams of two or three students. This size is ideal for attaining maximum accountability and involvement.

2. Hand out the reproducible and review each of the sections to be completed together as a class.

3. Require *every* team member to provide written evidence that he or she has actively participated by writing on the activity worksheet.

4. To ensure that all teams complete the activity within a given time frame, state upfront the minimum points that you expect teams to achieve and cue students when to move on; for example, say, "You have been working on the activity for 10 minutes. Your group should now be working on section 2. If you're not at this point, then you will need to work a little more quickly." This helps students divide their time between the three sections (brainstorm, examine, apply or explain) more effectively.

5. As the first teams finish, discreetly ask them to write their discovered patterns on the board. This provides instructional material to teach from during the concluding discussion. If you find other groups begin to copy down any of this information, wait until all groups have finished before listing examples and explanations to discuss.

6. When the timer sounds, discuss the patterns that students have written on the board. By this point, most of the teams will have discovered the targeted pattern. When other language patterns are discovered, they may be emphasized along with the targeted pattern.

7. Have students set up a page in their notebooks titled "Word Patterns." After you have finished discussing the targeted pattern (and any others), students record what they have learned on the page, adding to it each time they complete an activity. Require students to record the patterns in their own words and give examples to help them better retain the information. Students use their notes to study for the Thinking Activity quizzes.

Reinforcing the Spelling Strategies

The purpose of these Thinking Activities is to highlight important word patterns that will help students to spell better. The instructional focus for these tasks needs to encourage students to work on their ability to notice and explain these language patterns. There is a close link between spelling patterns and spelling strategies. Look for opportunities to reinforce links to the spelling strategies as you teach these activities. Seize on teachable moments to reinforce spelling strategies such as rhyming, syllabication, word-in-word, and spelling–meaning connections.

Activity Scoring

Mark the activity worksheets using a 5-point scale for thought, detail, and how well students explain the discovered spelling pattern. The wide range of activity formats and the varying number of activity sections make it impossible to provide a one-size-fits-all marking format. Instead, consider each activity on a 5-point scale that places student work along a marking continuum: 5/5 being exceptional, 4/5 indicating good work, 3/5 reflecting satisfactory performance, 2/5 being work that needs improvement, and 1/5 reflecting work that is incomplete or below grade-level expectations. When assessing assignments using this scale, give points or partial points for each section students complete. Give more weight to the activity's final section because this is where students demonstrate what they have learned.

The Thinking Activities also can serve a secondary function of systematically teaching social skills, such as listening, not interrupting, encouraging others, not using put-downs, and learning how to divide work in an equitable manner. A quick and easy way to assess such skills is as follows:

1. Review the social skills you wish to emphasize prior to the activity.

2. Tell students that they will receive a number of additional points for working well together.

3. Emphasize that these points are theirs to keep or lose depending on how well they work within their groups.

4. Monitor each group's ability to demonstrate these social skills during the activity. Use your professional judgment to determine if any students have not earned these additional points.

5. After the activity's target pattern has been reviewed, debrief with students what worked well in their groups. Emphasize the social skills you want to develop in these discussions.

Teaching Tips

The following teaching tips apply to each of the Thinking Activities. Additional teaching tips are included in individual activities where applicable.

- When using cooperative groups, it is important to get the groups up and running quickly to set the tone for the lesson. Once most of the groups are on task, you will have time to support students who are having difficulty.

- Ask students to use "group hands" during the Thinking Activities to increase group self-reliance and maintain your own sanity. In a nutshell, "group hands" means that you only assist a team when all members have their hands raised.

- When reviewing the target pattern within each activity, be prepared for students to notice other useful patterns. Accept, discuss, and encourage these observations because they mean your students are beginning to think more critically about how words are built.

Special Needs Considerations

Most ELLs and students with learning difficulties are able to successfully complete the Thinking Activities with minimal support.

Working in cooperative groups can be especially beneficial for these students because they do not have to know all the answers. When assigned as individual assignments, some students will have a little more difficulty, but most are still able to complete the task at their own level of functioning. In general terms, students find the brainstorming part of these activities easy. The examination of the words may be moderately difficult, and the application or explanation of the language pattern may be challenging. For students who run into difficulty, consider providing additional instruction to emphasize important categories and/or patterns (e.g., listening to vowel sounds, noticing particular letter patterns). Often some concrete examples, or a little hint, can go a long way to helping students to better understand and refocus. Adapt the activities as required for students who have special needs when these activities are assigned as individual tasks. Specifically, consider reducing the number of questions or sections assigned for students who struggle with written output issues.

Quiz Administration

In addition to scoring each activity, a way to evaluate student progress is to periodically test students on their retention of targeted language patterns. The Reproducibles section of this book provides three quizzes, one to follow each set of Thinking Activities. The quizzes measure students' study skills, spelling strategy knowledge, and understanding of targeted language patterns.

Advance Preparation

Prior to the test date for any of the quizzes, review the target spelling patterns together as a class. This review provides students a final opportunity to clarify questions and add any information that they may have missed. Remind students to also review the Spelling Strategies Diagram so they are prepared to answer questions relating to the strategies. Tell them that they will need to be prepared to explain each spelling pattern and to provide examples.

Quiz Format

Each quiz will require approximately 20–30 minutes and can be completed under normal testing conditions. Ensure that students have proper writing materials, are separated from their peers, and are working in a quiet classroom environment. When students are finished, collect and mark the quizzes.

Quiz Scoring

Mark Quiz 1 out of 15 points. Assign 9 points to questions 1–7, which measure student knowledge of the target spelling patterns. In these questions, each answer receives 1 point and the examples in questions 1 and 3 each receive an additional point, for a total of 9. Assign 6 points to questions 8–10. These questions measure student strategy knowledge. Students should receive 1 point for question 8, 3 points for question 9, and 2 points for question 10.

Mark Quiz 2 out of 15 points. Assign 1 point to all questions except numbers 2, 4, and 5. Mark these questions out of 2 points because they require additional explanation.

Quiz 3 should also be marked out of 15 points. Assign 1 point to questions 2, 3, 7, 8, and 10. Mark questions 1, 4, 5, 6, and 9 out of 2 points each because these require greater explanation.

Special Needs Considerations

Some students with special needs will find the range of material they need to recall and the open-ended nature of the test questions challenging. They can often explain the spelling strategies but struggle to recall the target spelling patterns. To better support these learners, consider allowing them to use their notes, reducing the total score of their test, or having someone discuss and/or scribe answers.

How Short and Long Get Along

THINKING ACTIVITIES
Vowels

Students are given a great deal of instruction about long and short vowels in the primary grades to help them learn to read. In the middle grades, students often no longer consciously think about vowel sounds, yet vowels are important spelling clues. To help students become more conscious of how vowel sounds influence word spellings, use this activity along with the Thinking Activities The Magic *e* and When Two Vowels Go Walking, and the Pattern Activities Rhyme Time and Word Association.

This activity examines the difference between long and short vowels: Long vowel sounds say their own name (e.g., in *cane, bite, boat, cute, meet*) and short vowel sounds are much more brief (e.g., in *can, sit, hot, cup, bet*). It is important that students know the difference between long and short vowels because many letter patterns are influenced by them in multisyllable words.

Materials

• Reproducible 9, How Short and Long Get Along

Advance Preparation

Photocopy Reproducible 9 and select words to use as examples of short and long vowel sounds. Consider using words from recent units or lessons in other subject areas.

Lesson Format

Objective: Students will be able to recognize and differentiate long and short vowel sounds and letter patterns.

Procedure:

1. Discuss with students prior to the activity the difference between long and short vowel sounds. Tell them these vowel sounds are important indicators of some spelling patterns in multisyllable words. Emphasize that long vowel sounds say their own name while short vowel sounds make a much more brief sound.

2. Practice several examples with students to reinforce the concept. A fun, interactive method to practice the difference between long and short vowel sounds is to play an action game. Simply ask students to stand up and listen to the vowel sounds within the words you call out. If the word possesses a long vowel sound, the students stretch upward. If it is a short vowel sound, they squat downward. This quick and lively activity is an excellent way to reinforce the different vowel sounds and can be done almost anywhere!

3. Complete the remainder of this activity using the general procedures outlined earlier in this chapter (see page 49). At the conclusion of the activity, ask students to record what they have learned about this word pattern within their Word Patterns page. Students will need to refer back to this sheet to study for Thinking Activity quizzes.

Activity Scoring

Mark this activity using the previously discussed 5-point scale. Consider assigning 3 points for question 1 and 2 points for question 2. In question 1, deduct a half-point for each box in the chart that is incomplete or inaccurate. In question 2, each sentence is worth 1 point if completed in a satisfactory manner.

The Magic e

The Magic *e* reviews how vowels can make either long or short vowel sounds. Long vowels tend to occur when words either end with an *e* or when two vowels are placed beside one another in a word. Short vowels tend to occur when words do not end with an *e* or when the vowel is boxed in by two consonants. During this activity, reinforce

- the difference between long and short vowel sounds,

- how silent *e* at the end of a word creates a long vowel sound for the inner vowel, and

- the importance of dropping the silent *e* when adding a suffix to a word.

This last point is especially important because it establishes a predictable spelling step students can use when adding suffixes to words. Without this clarification, students may believe that there are exceptions to the rule; for example, they may believe that if a word ends with *e* that they just add *d*. By teaching students that the silent *e* is always dropped, you clarify for students that suffixes are spelled in particular ways because of their meanings.

Materials

- Reproducible 10, The Magic *e*

Lesson Format

Objective: Students will be able to recognize the difference between long and short vowel sounds and, specifically, how a silent *e* at the end of words with a vowel/consonant/vowel pattern creates a long vowel sound.

Procedure:

1. Reinforce the concept of long and short vowel sounds using the vowel-sound game introduced in the previous activity.

2. Review with the class what happens when suffixes are added to words ending with a silent *e*. Provide several examples using *-ing* and *-ed* to illustrate that silent *e* is always dropped before a suffix is added.

3. Introduce, assign, and monitor student progress using Reproducible 10.

4. Collect Reproducible 10 and review with your class what word patterns they noticed. In this discussion, emphasize the target spelling pattern. Ask students to place an explanation of this silent *e* spelling pattern and concrete examples within their notebooks' Word Patterns page.

Create a Language

For some students, reading dictionary definitions is like trying to understand a foreign language. They struggle to understand how words are presented and explained. This activity helps students to become a little more comfortable when using a dictionary. It reviews how to read and understand dictionary definitions with extension activities that require the students to apply this knowledge by creating their own silly dictionary definitions.

Materials

- Reproducible 11, Create a Language

Advance Preparation

Preview the instructional steps within the lesson: alphabetization, a basic dictionary word-definition framework, and how students will create dictionary definitions. Preselect a few basic word definitions from the dictionary to use as instructional examples.

Lesson Format

Time Required: Approximately 45 minutes.

Objective: Students will demonstrate an understanding of a basic dictionary definition by creating their own "silly" dictionary definitions.

Procedure

1. Review the basics of how to read a dictionary definition. Examine some dictionary entries to emphasize main features such as

   - how to use the guide words at the top of each page

   - how alphabetization is used to list the words in order, starting with the first letter, then the second letter, and so on.

2. Practice this alphabetization skill using the word families listed below. Ask your students to sort each word family into alphabetical order. For syllabication practice, also ask your students to divide each word into syllables, using bullet points like a dictionary would (e.g., *al·pha·bet·i·cal*). When they are finished, ask them what patterns they notice within and between the word families. Use this discussion to emphasize that words with similar meanings (root word) often have similar spellings (spelling–meaning connection).

   farm, farmyard, farmhand, farmstead, farming, farmland

   pass, passerby, passage, passbook, passable, passenger

   cloth, clothes, clothespin, clothier, clothespress, clothing

   rough, roughhouse, roughshod, roughneck, roughen, roughhewn

3. Next, to better teach your students how to read, and create, their own dictionary definitions, teach them the basic framework for a word definition:

   1. word divided into syllables (using bullet points),

   2. word definition(s),

   3. sentence to show meaning, and

   4. word with common suffixes such as *-ed* and *-ing* to show past and present tenses.

   In this instruction also be sure to discuss how some words can have multiple meanings or spellings (*colour/color, neighbour/neighbor*) because of where the word origi-

THINKING ACTIVITIES
Vowels

54

nated. Words from languages such as Greek, Latin, Old English, French, and Spanish are all found within the English language.

4. Have students create their own word and dictionary definitions, such as

Sprickles—a very very happy feeling.

i.e., I'm feeling spricklish today.

sprickled, sprickling, spricklish

Teaching Tips

• If your students have difficulty creating their own words, help them to create their own word possibilities using Greek and Latin roots. To play, ask the students to brainstorm and write 3–5 interesting root words. Then give them some of the Greek or Latin prefixes to go in front of the root words, such as *mono-, sub-, therm-, astr-, dent-, opt-, grat-,* or *chron-*. Students then choose their favorite sounding word to use.

• This activity provides a good opportunity to quickly review with students some of the add and drop rules discussed within the Pattern Activities that apply to the ends of words when adding suffixes.

• To increase the difficulty level, challenge your stronger students to create two meanings for their words or use *n, v,* or *adj* to indicate whether their new word is a noun, verb, or adjective.

Extension: Silly Words in Action!

If time permits, consider extending this activity into a short story or poem assignment incorporating students' silly words, or make a class list of these invented words and agree to use them in a skit or as part of class conversations for a day.

When Two Vowels Go Walking

When Two Vowels Go Walking gets students to think more deeply about the interactions between vowels. Students cannot be successful spellers by only sounding out words. They need to use a variety of strategies. Phonetic patterns do play an important role in initially teaching students to read and write; for example, teachers of the primary grades often teach the two-vowel pattern for single-syllable words: When two vowels are placed beside each other, the first vowel is the only one heard, and it is a long vowel. Often, teachers use the following mnemonic to help students remember the rule:

When two vowels go walking,

the first one does the talking

and says its own name.

The two-vowel pattern is useful for teaching early reading skills. Unfortunately, it is not a reliable strategy for spelling multisyllable words. In a classic study, Theodore Clymer (1963) reviewed four widely used primary readers for the most common vowel digraphs. He found that the two-vowel pattern was reliable only about two-thirds of the time:

- 97% of the time for *oa* words

- 66% of the time for *ea* words

- 64% of the time for *ai* words

The two-vowel pattern was not very reliable for *ie* or *ui* words. This two-vowel sound pattern should be one of the things students consider when attempting to spell. It should not, however, be the only type of information they use. Good spellers use sound, meaning, and visual information when spelling. Emphasize with students that this activity shows why they cannot rely on sound alone when spelling.

Materials

- photocopies of Reproducible 12, When Two Vowels Go Walking (one for each team)

- dictionaries (one for each team)

Lesson Format

Objective: Students will demonstrate an understanding of what happens when two vowels are presented together in one-syllable words. They will also be able to recognize that this pattern is not consistent in many multisyllable words.

Procedure:

1. Complete this activity using the general procedures outlined earlier in this chapter (see page 49).

2. At the conclusion of the activity, ask students to record on the Word Patterns page of their notebooks what they have learned about this word pattern.

Teaching Tips

Some students may not be familiar with the term *multisyllable word* and may need a quick explanation. To better illustrate this term, consider clapping out the syllables of a few multisyllable words to better show these individual syllable units.

Extension: Researching Word Patterns

If time permits, consider extending this activity into a scientific research/graphing lesson. See if your students attain results that are the same (or different) from Clymer (1963). In his study, this phonetic two-vowel pattern was more reliable for some two-vowel combinations than it was for others. Students can replicate his study by using short, single-syllable words from primary readers, textbooks, or novels. (Use five categories: *oa, ai, ea, ie, ei.*) Then compare the class's results to Clymer's. It provides a great opportunity to discuss the pattern, the scientif- ic method, and your students' theories about why their findings were the same or different than the original study.

Sneaky Sounds

To spell multisyllable words accurately, students need to understand that different letter combinations can make the same sound. Sneaky Sounds stimulates student analysis and discussion rather than focusing on specific rules or patterns. It visually shows students that combining sounding out with other strategies is the best way to understand alphabet patterns (letter–sound correspondence), word-in-word patterns, and spelling–meaning connections (Henderson & Templeton, 1986).

Materials

• dictionaries (one per student)

Lesson Format

Objective: Students will explain why they need to use a range of strategies, and not just sound, to accurately spell multisyllable words.

Procedure:

1. Have students brainstorm words that have letter combinations that make the /f/ sound (e.g., *free, phone, tough, rough, fried, frog, enough, stuff, fluff*). Prompt students with a few hints to help them find any they have difficulty with.

2. Ask, "What patterns do you notice? Are there letter combinations that only make the /f/ sound in a certain part of the word (i.e., beginning, middle, end)?" If students have difficulty highlighting patterns, point out that *gh* and *ff* only make the /f/ sound at the end of words. Students may then notice other patterns such as how *ph* usually makes the /f/ sound at the beginning of words, or that you infrequently see a word that ends with only one *f*.

3. Have a class contest to see how many different ways the /k/ and /sh/ sounds can be spelled. Frame it as an individual or group "beat the clock" brainstorming game. Ask students to record the answers in their notebooks. Allow students to search for approximately three minutes, and encourage them to scan their dictionaries for potential words. Some possible answers are as follows:

/k/

kite, cake, torque, deck, chrome, fax, occupy

/sh/

shoe, cache, ratio, sure, racial, Russian

4. Discuss with students the patterns they notice. Ask, "Do some letter combinations only make a particular sound when in a certain part of the word [i.e., beginning, middle, end]?"

5. Ask students to respond in their notebooks to the prompts "Why did we do this activity today? What did this activity teach us? Describe one interesting spelling pattern you noticed today." Tell students this written work will be evaluated on their thought, detail, and presentation.

Reinforcing the Spelling Strategies

This activity contains many teachable moments that can be used to draw student attention to Spelling Strategies. For example, some words used to demonstrate the /k/ and /sh/ sounds can also be used to review the following:

• spelling–meaning connections (e.g., *racial/racism/racist, shoe/shoelace/shoemaker/shoestring*)

• doubling issues (e.g., *Rus·sian* and *oc·cu·pan·cy* show how syllable breaks split double consonants)

- dropping/adding issues with affixes (e.g., in *occupied* the *y* is dropped and *i* is added; in *caked* the *e* is dropped and *ed* is added)
- letter patterns determined by rhyming (e.g., *deck* can be rhymed with *neck, check, peck, wreck*; *chrome* can be rhymed with *home, dome, roam, foam* [this second example provides an opportunity to discuss how not all sound patterns contain just one dominant pattern])

Activity Scoring

Mark this activity using the 5-point scale outlined earlier in this chapter. Pay particular attention to how well students express their ideas. Do their answers demonstrate an understanding of the problems that occur if they rely only on sound to spell? Do their answers contain sufficient explanatory detail? Are they written in a clear manner?

Teaching Tips

Try to present this activity as an interesting brainstorming activity. Students respond well to this task if it is presented as something they are discovering *with* you.

Special Needs Considerations

Students who have special needs often find the brainstorming of various letter–sound combinations difficult. Consider quietly reviewing the important points of the lesson a second time and reducing the number of questions to be completed. Make notes of any key words students mention in conversation with you within their notebooks. This will provide them with a reference once you have left.

Extension: Sorting Sounds

This activity format can be used to create additional sorting activities for any problematic sound-based language patterns. Simply ask students to generate a list of words that follow the target sound. Then have them separate the list words into categories based on which letter combinations created the sound (e.g., the long /a/ sound can be made by *a, ei, ay, ai*). It is useful to include a final category called "other" to help organize any additional patterns students find.

Is It ei or ie?

Whether to use *ei* or *ie* in a word often can be predicted based on the sound these letters make. When words make a long /a/ sound, they are usually spelled *ei*. If words make an long *e* sound they are often spelled with *ie*. A third interesting pattern students often detect is that it is usually only in short three-letter words (e.g., *lie, die*) that this pattern makes a long /i/ sound.

Materials

• photocopies of Reproducible 13, Is It *ei* or *ie*? (one for each team)

Lesson Format

Objective: Students will be able to determine when to use *ei* or *ie* by the sound these vowel combinations make.

Procedure:

1. Complete this activity using the general procedures outlined earlier in this chapter (see page 49).

2. At the conclusion of the activity, ask students to record on the Word Patterns page of their notebooks what they have learned about this word pattern.

Vowel Variations

Vowel Variations is a cooperative categorization activity that gets students actively comparing, examining, and saying vowel sounds. All of the activity words contain the vowel *a* (either alone or with another vowel) in order to show how many patterns there are in the English language with just this one letter. The activity reinforces the use of a range of spelling strategies; the importance of sound, visual cues, and meaning in spelling; and some specific overlapping language patterns that students need to know in order to read.

Materials

- photocopies of Reproducible 14, Vowel Variations (one for each team)
- scissors (one pair for each team)
- construction paper (one sheet for each team)
- markers (one for each team)
- glue (one container for each team)

Lesson Format

Time Required: Approximately 45–60 minutes.

Objective: Students will cooperatively discuss, compare, and categorize words based upon the vowel sounds within the words.

Procedure:

1. Hand out photocopies of Reproducible 14 to the teams and ask them to
   - cut out the words,
   - categorize them into different groups based on their vowel sounds, and
   - create a heading for each category based on the vowel sound.

2. Before they begin the activity, have the student teams discuss how to divide the workload fairly to ensure that everyone is thinking and writing equally.

3. When the teams have generated their categories, have them explain why the categories make sense.

4. Provide each team with a sheet of construction paper and ask them to write the names of team members in marker on the back and the category headings across the top of the front.

5. Have students glue each word under the appropriate category heading, leaving one inch across the bottom to complete a final summarizing task.

6. When students are finished sorting and gluing their words into the categories, have them answer this question in the one-inch strip across the bottom of the worksheet: "What have you noticed about the vowels and their sounds?" Most teams will realize that each vowel can make several sounds, depending on how it is used in a word.

7. When all the teams have finished, discuss students' observations. If not already mentioned, draw attention to the fact that all the words examined used only the vowel *a* (either alone or with another vowel). During this discussion, highlight how students could use their spelling strategies to help spell these words. Pay particular attention to how many of these words can be expanded to create numerous other related words.

8. Collect the activity for marking.

Teaching Tips

To incorporate more categorizing into this task consider beginning with an "open" sort where students determine the category headings the words fall under. This twist can generate some interesting conversation.

Fat or Skinny CaKe?

Fat or Skinny CaKe? explains how to tell whether a word beginning with a /k/ sound should start with a *c* or a *k*. If the vowel after the /k/ sound is fat (*a, o, u*) then the word usually starts with a *c*. If the vowel is skinny (*i, e*) the word begins with a *k*.

Materials

• photocopies of Reproducible 15, Fat or Skinny CaKe? (one for each team)

Lesson Format

Objective: Students will be able to use vowel sounds to explain whether a word beginning with a /k/ sound should start with a *c* or a *k*.

Procedure:

1. Complete this activity using the general procedures outlined earlier in this chapter (see page 49).

2. At the conclusion of the activity ask students to record on the Word Patterns page of their notebooks what they have learned about this word pattern.

Crack the Code

Crack the Code explains when to use a *ck* or *k* in the middle and at the end of words. Generally, if you hear a consonant before the /k/ sound, you use the letter *k* alone. If you hear a vowel before the /k/ sound, however, the pattern is most often *ck*.

Materials

- photocopies of Reproducible 16, Crack the Code (one for each team)

Lesson Format

Objective: Students will know whether to use *ck* or *k* in the middle or end of a word by looking at the preceding letter.

Procedure:

1. Complete this activity using the general procedures outlined earlier in this chapter (see page 49).

2. At the conclusion of the activity ask students to record on the Word Patterns page of their notebooks what they have learned about this word pattern.

Teaching Tips

Use this activity to further highlight rhyming and spelling–meaning connections by asking them to rhyme and/or expand some of the words they have used.

Homonym Headaches

Homonyms (words that sound the same, are spelled differently, and have different meanings) are frequently misspelled by middle school students. This is likely because the human brain stores and accesses words by using both sound and meaning cues to recall words (Moats, 1995). To accurately recall the correct spellings of homonyms, the brain has to sort out that the same *sound* (e.g., *their/there*) has more than one spelling and more than one meaning.

Materials

- photocopies of Reproducible 17, Homonym Poem (one for each student)

- photocopies of Reproducible 18, Homonym Headaches (one for each student)

Lesson Format

Time Required: Approximately 1 hour to complete both reproducible worksheets. Consider splitting this task into two 30-minute lessons to maximize student interest and retention.

Objective: Students will demonstrate an understanding of what a homonym is and develop some personal spelling strategies to better spell the most troublesome ones.

Procedure:

1. Hand out photocopies of Reproducible 17 to be completed as an individual assignment.

2. Discuss as a class what makes a homonym and generate a long class list of these words. Encourage students to look in the dictionary for additional homonym pairs. This class list will help students to better notice the homonyms when completing the reproducibles.

3. Ask students to complete Reproducible 17; then mark the worksheet together as a class.

4. Assign Reproducible 18. Encourage students to fill in section 1 with pairs of homonyms that have been troublesome or confusing in the past.

5. Ask students to select a specified number of pairs of these homonyms to examine further.

6. Discuss how students might be able to better remember the homonyms by artificially attaching a meaning to them; for example, to remember the homonyms *which* and *witch*, students can imagine that a broomstick (*t*) is carried by a *witch*.

7. Have students create personal clues for their homonyms and list them on the worksheet.

8. Ask students to share their homonym clues in partners and then as a whole class.

9. Ask students to explain the three things a word must possess to be considered a homonym in their notebook's Word Patterns page. Remind students to include adequate detail and examples because these entries will be their study notes for the quizzes.

10. Collect Reproducible 18 for marking.

Extension: Write Makes Right!

The best way to get these troublesome homonyms right is to have students use them more consistently in their writing. For additional practice with troublesome homonyms ask students to incorporate a number of these homonym pairs into writing assignments.

- Using the Spelling Stories activity outlined in chapter 5, have students create a short paragraph misspelling their homonyms. Below this first paragraph, students write the corrected paragraph with the corrections underlined. Select a few of the best misspelled homonym paragraphs. Over the next few days, have the class spend 10 minutes per day writing the stories in their notebooks and editing them. They can be quickly marked together as a class.

- Have students use their chosen homonyms two or three times in a silly story or rhyming poem.

- Assign a homonym homework challenge in which students try to create the largest list of homonym pairs in the class.

Ch, tch, cha!

This activity examines whether to use *tch* or *ch*. To determine this pattern, look at the letters preceding these letter combinations. If a vowel (often *a* or *i*) is heard before the /ch/ sound, the word is most often spelled with a *tch*; if a consonant (often *n*) is heard before the /ch/ sound, the word is generally spelled with *ch*. This pattern is very similar to the one for words ending in a /k/ sound (Crack the Code). In both of these patterns, the letter preceding the letter combinations provides a good indication of what will follow. When a /k/ or /ch/ sound is preceded by

- a consonant, the letters *k* or *ch* will often follow;

- a vowel, the letters *tch* and *ck* come next.

Materials

- photocopies of Reproducible 19, Ch, tch, cha!

Lesson Format

Objective: Students will be able to explain whether to use *tch* or *ch* within a variety of words by observing the preceding letter.

Procedure:

1. Complete this activity using the general procedures outlined earlier in this chapter (see page 49).

2. At the conclusion of the activity, ask students to record on the Word Patterns page of their notebooks what they have learned about this word pattern.

Teaching Tips

This activity works better as a small-group task because it is a little more challenging. The final two questions in this activity both require students to explain underlying spelling patterns. If students have difficulty with either of these final two questions, refer them back to the visual cues within the question. In question 3, discuss what the "hint" is trying to highlight. In question 4, examine the word examples provided, and refer students back to their Word Patterns pages to review what they wrote about the *k* or *ck* pattern.

Predictable Patterns

Predictable Patterns reviews two common patterns found in multisyllable words: the *-able/-ible* suffix and the /shun/ suffix. Whether to use the Latin-based suffix *-able* or *-ible* can be predicted by looking at the root word. If the root can be read as a word by itself, then use *-able* (e.g., *profit + able = profitable*; *afford + able = affordable*). If the root cannot stand by itself, the suffix is often *-ible* (e.g., *terr + ible = terrible*; *invinc + ible = invincible*). Although there are a variety of letter combinations that make the /shun/ sound, most words that end in this sound are formed with the suffix *-tion*.

These two predictable, easy-to-learn suffix patterns are often not taught explicitly, yet "an essential part of understanding how words are constructed involves recognizing that many words share common and predictable letter sequences. Studying word families and discussing their similarities and differences has always been an important activity in this respect" (Westwood, 1999, p. 4). In this activity, students review word families to discover predictable patterns they can use when spelling multisyllable words.

Materials

- photocopies of Reproducible 20, Predictable Patterns (one for each person)
- dictionaries (one for each person)

Lesson Format

Time Required: Approximately 20 minutes.

Objective: Students will be able to explain when to use *-tion* versus *-shun* and *-able* versus *-ible*.

Procedure:

1. Complete this activity using the general procedures outlined earlier in this chapter (see page 49).

2. At the conclusion of the activity, ask students to record on the Word Patterns page of their notebooks what they have learned about this word pattern.

Teaching Tips

- The simple format and the consistent nature of the activity's two patterns make this a good individual task.

- Encourage students to use the dictionary when brainstorming this word list. If anyone experiences difficulty finding enough words, brainstorm some good examples as a class. This will ensure that everyone has enough words to make an informed comparison.

- Use the multisyllable words within this activity to practice syllabication, highlight smaller words within larger ones, and discuss spelling–meaning connections.

Extension: Pleasant Pattern Practice

To provide additional practice, assign a writing assignment to contrast *-able* and *-ible*, or to emphasize *-tion*. Possible assignments could be to complete an exaggerated spelling story as outlined in chapter 5; to create word-search puzzles using the suffix patterns, then photocopy the best ones and share them with the whole class; or to have a class contest to see who can find the most examples for each pattern. Students love this, especially if you make it into a challenge.

Prefixes and Suffixes Poster

Students need many opportunities to examine how multisyllable words go together. This activity combines spelling and art to provide students with another chance to review prefixes and suffixes. It is a good example of how spelling instruction can be incorporated across the curriculum.

Materials

- dictionaries (one for each team)
- timer
- white poster paper (8.5 × 11-inch paper works well)
- colored pencils and/or markers

Lesson Format

Time Required: Approximately 75 minutes.

Objective: Students will be able to demonstrate an understanding of how common prefixes and suffixes combine with root words.

Procedure:

1. Discuss how many words have patterned beginnings (prefixes) and patterned endings (suffixes). Ask students to brainstorm common prefixes and suffixes (e.g., *un-*, *pre-*, *-ment*, *-ing*). Make the brainstorm into a game in which teams race against the clock and one another to find the most examples. Encourage teams to use dictionaries.

2. Ask students why they think prefixes and suffixes have become part of the English language. Why are they needed? These are common responses:

- Affixes are a logical way to create new words from a common root.
- Affixes allow writers to change tense (past, present, future), to make plurals, and to make opposites.

3. Have each individual student make a poster that lists prefixes and suffixes according to the scoring guideline. These posters should provide the reader with an explanation of what prefixes and suffixes are, present a range of examples, and include adequate color, illustrations, and creativity.

Teaching Tip

Highlight how to add and drop letters when using affixes during your classroom discussion.

Activity Scoring

When marking this activity, consider evaluating it out of 15 points using the following criteria:

- 5 points for prefix/suffix definitions and an eye-catching title
- 5 points for various prefixes and suffixes presented on the poster
- 5 points for presentation (color, creativity, designs, or illustrations)

Extension: Monster Words!

A fun extension activity is to hold a class contest to see who can find the longest or strangest words that use prefixes and suffixes.

Y Endings Are Easy

This activity highlights two important patterns for words ending with -y. First, in many multisyllable words, -y makes a long /e/ sound (e.g., *happily*, *crazily*, *constantly*). Some students mistakenly place an *e* at the end of these words because it is the sound they hear. It is important that they consider not only sound but also visual cues and meaning patterns. Second, students are often unsure whether to add -*ally* or -*ly* when they are spelling long -y words. Teach students to use -*ly* unless the root word ends in -*ic*. It is mainly -*ic* root words that tend to be formed using -*ally* (e.g., *logically* and *frantically*).

Materials

- photocopies of Reproducible 21, *Y Endings Are Easy*

- dictionaries (one for each student or team)

Advance Preparation

Decide whether this will be completed as an individual or team activity.

Lesson Format

Objective: Students will be able to explain when to use the suffixes -*ly* and -*ally*.

Procedure:

1. Complete this activity using the general procedures outlined earlier in this chapter (see page 49).

2. At the conclusion of the activity, ask students to record on the Word Patterns page of their notebooks what they have learned about this word pattern.

Teaching Tips

This activity provides a good opportunity to discuss how root words form the basis of dictionary definitions. It is an important conversation because not all students realize that, in order to find a word (e.g., *scientifically*), they often need to find the root word (*science*). Words with the suffixes -*ly* or -*ally* are often listed in bold after the definition of the root word because they only slightly change the word's basic meaning (e.g., *crazy* versus *crazily*). In some cases, however, a suffix can significantly change the meaning of a word (e.g., *slipper* versus *slippery*). In these cases, the words are listed in the dictionary with their own definitions. Challenge students to find other examples of words that are listed separately from their root words in their dictionaries.

THINKING ACTIVITIES
Homonyms/Syllabication/Affixes

The Vanishing e

The Vanishing *e* reviews what happens to words ending in silent *e* when suffixes are added. In this task, the silent *e* is dropped before the suffixes *-ed* or *-ing* can be added. When making these words plural, the *s* is just added with no change to the silent *e*.

Materials

• photocopies of Reproducible 22, The Vanishing *e*

• dictionaries (one for each team)

Lesson Format

Objective: Students will be able to explain what happens in words ending in a silent *e* when the suffixes *-ed*, *-ing*, and *-s* are added.

Procedure:

1. Complete this activity using the general procedures outlined earlier in this chapter (see page 49).

2. At the conclusion of the activity, ask students to record on the Word Patterns page of their notebooks what they have learned about this word pattern.

Teaching Tip

Include within your introduction a brief review of where to find words with suffixes. Some students will forget to look for these derivatives beneath the root word's definition if you don't remind them.

Become an Etymologist

Etymologists study the history of words. They trace the development and relationships of words within our language. In this activity, students take on the role of etymologists and examine how several Greek and Latin roots have been incorporated into our present-day English language.

Materials

- photocopies of Reproducible 23, Become an Etymologist (one for each person)

- dictionaries (one for each person)

Lesson Format

Objective: Students will become more aware of how word history and meaning impact the spelling of many words.

Procedure:

1. Discuss with students how words from other languages, such as Greek, Latin, Old English, French, German, and Spanish, are all found within the modern English language.

2. Create a class list of words that are part of the modern English language but "probably" originated elsewhere. Treat this as a brainstorming session. Do not feel you need to verify the origin of every word. The origin of some words, such as baguette (French), may be obvious but others will not. The purpose of this step is merely to pique student curiosity about these word meanings. Ask students to scan their dictionaries to find words that have come from other languages. Encourage them to guess as to the possible origin of these words.

3. Introduce and assign Reproducible 23 as an individual assignment.

4. Mark and review this activity as a class. Be sure to ask students to record what they have learned upon their Word Patterns page at the conclusion of the activity.

5. Collect Reproducible 23 to record points.

Activity Scoring

Mark this activity out of 5 points. Assign 4 points for how well students complete the chart, and 1 point for question 2. Within the chart, deduct a half mark for every box that students do not complete accurately. In question 2, accept any reasonable answers concerning what this activity teaches us about words. Some common answers are that

- there are many words within our language that have come from other languages;

- there are many spelling–meaning connections between words; and

- there are many spelling–meaning connections that we don't always notice.

Teaching Tips

- This activity works best as an individual assignment.

- Use some of the words to highlight how the meaning of a word changes when prefixes are added or removed.

Extension: Expanding Words

- Students benefit from additional practice to help them notice Latin and Greek spelling–meaning connections. Consider using the Latin or Greek prefixes listed within this assignment as starter words for the Expanding Words Pattern Activity. For example, from *sign*, students can brainstorm related words such as *signals, signature, signboard,* or *significance.* Encourage students to use their dictionaries to find even more connections.

- Ask students to use several of the words listed within the reproducible in an exaggerated paragraph. Start with something truthful and then exaggerate until the events are ridiculous. When students are finished, ask them to go back and underline the Latin or Greek roots. To increase the difficulty, ask them to only use one or two roots in their paragraphs, and insist that they include a number of related words (spelling–meaning connections).

ing Endings

This activity reviews what occurs at the ends of words when the suffix *-ing* is added. It examines when to double letters, drop letters, or add the suffix with no change to the root word. In particular, it highlights how students can often use a short vowel sound before a consonant as an indicator that the letter needs to be doubled.

Materials

- photocopies of Reproducible 24, *ing* Endings
- dictionaries (one or two for each team)

Lesson Format

Objective: Students will know to double the final consonant in a word when adding a suffix if the letter preceding is a short vowel.

Procedure:

1. Complete this activity using the general procedures outlined earlier in this chapter (see page 49).

2. At the conclusion of the activity, ask students to record on the Word Patterns page of their notebooks what they have learned about this word pattern.

Spelling Variations

Materials

- photocopies of Reproducible 25, Spelling Variations (one for each student)
- dictionaries (one for each student)

Lesson Format

Time Required: Approximately 45 minutes.

Objective: Students will be able to recognize some of the more common variations in word spellings between the United States and Canada.

Procedure:

1. Discuss with your class how the English language has been influenced by many different cultures. It has meant that some words have evolved to have more than one correct spelling. Even between Canada and the United States subtle spelling differences exist because Canada was a British colony far longer.

2. Brainstorm a class list of words with two different spellings. Use this list to discuss the three main differences between American and Canadian spellings:

   Main Canadian/American Spelling Differences

   1. *our* versus *or*   *colour/color* or *neighbour/neighbor*

   2. *s* versus *z*   *summarise/summarize* or *recognise/recognize*

   3. *re* versus *er*   *centre/center* or *metre/meter*

3. Use the dictionary to examine words with multiple spellings. This helps students to see how the dictionary lists these words. To ensure this lesson works well consider

   - setting a specific time limit for work completion (20 minutes works well);
   - insisting that students use no more than two word pairs from any one page;
   - assigning a minimum number of words students must find for each category;
   - telling students you have decided on a "secret" number of word pairs they must find to achieve full marks. Do not tell them this number prior to the completion of the activity.

4. Place students in small working groups and distribute Reproducible 25.

5. Review the four categories within the chart: *our* versus *or*, *s* versus *z*, *re* versus *er*, and Other Patterns. Explain that the Other Patterns category is for students to list word pairs that do not fit into the other sections.

6. Ask students to begin the activity, and monitor progress.

7. Review the activity as a class. Discuss with students if they think these spelling differences between Canada, the United States, and other English-speaking countries will always remain? Consider that

   - languages never stay the same because new words are invented and old words are forgotten;
   - the invention of new technologies, such as computers, has added a number of new words to our language.

   Using computers as an example, ask your class if they can think of any relatively new words or new meanings for existing words (e.g., *Internet, computer mouse, chat room*).

8. To mark, ask students to exchange worksheets and count up the total number of word pairs on the sheet. List a 5-point marking scale on the board indicating how many word pairs students need to attain a certain score. Have students hand back the marked assignment, and then collect to record the results.

9. Ask students to explain the differences between Canadian and American word spellings in their Word Patterns page.

Activity Scoring

Mark this activity using a 5-point scale. Assign student scores based on the number of word pairs found (i.e., 15 or more pairs of words are worth 3/5 and 20 or more pairs of words are worth 4/5). Monitor student progress during the activity to determine the number of pairs students need to find to attain a certain score.

Teaching Tips

• Place your students in "working groups" to help them to locate the words more efficiently. Frame the game as a "beat the clock" race where students need to work together to find as many word pair examples as they can within the given time frame.

• This activity provides an excellent format to review social skills such as good listening, not interrupting, encouraging others, not using put-downs, and learning how to divide work in a equitable manner. For additional information, refer to the general teaching tips presented earlier in this chapter.

You're the Judge

You're the Judge examines why consonants often need to be doubled after short vowel sounds. Knowing whether or not to double consonants within multisyllable words is an ongoing struggle for many middle-grade students. Henderson (1990) refers to this understanding as the core principle of the Syllable Juncture stage. It is also a very teachable concept. This task reinforces with students how they can use short vowel sounds before a consonant to determine if a letter needs to be doubled.

Materials

• Reproducible 26, You're the Judge

Lesson Format

Objective: Students will be able to explain how the vowel sound preceding a letter can indicate whether or not the letter should be doubled.

Procedure:

1. Complete this activity using the general procedures outlined earlier in this chapter (see page 49).

2. At the conclusion of the activity, ask students to record on the Word Patterns page of their notebooks what they have learned about this word pattern.

Teaching Tips

• This activity can be completed as a collaborative group task, but its relatively straightforward format makes it an ideal individual assignment.

• This activity is ideal for reviewing syllabication. Remind students that when they are not sure if a letter should be doubled, they can always use syllabication. Twinned letters are consistently split by syllable breaks (e.g., fun·nel, shal·low).

Linking Letters

When a suffix is added, many root words drop or replace their last letter; for example *lady* changes to *ladies* (the *y* changes to *i*), and *carve* changes to *carving* (the *e* is dropped). This pattern of dropping and replacing letters also happens in the middle of multisyllable words; for example *reproduce* becomes *reproduction* (the *e* is dropped), and *multiply* becomes *multiplication* (the *y* becomes *i*). With this activity, teach students that the changeable letters in the middle of long, multisyllable words are linking letters.

Advance Preparation

Prior to teaching this lesson, write the Linking Letters examples on an overhead or board to minimize student wait time.

Lesson Format

Objective: Students will be able to identify the letters most often dropped and substituted in multisyllable words ending in *-tion*.

Procedure:

1. Teach students about linking letters using the following examples.

   reproduce + tion = reproduction

   direct + tion = direction

   imagine + tion = imagination

   monopolize + tion = monopolization

   multiply becomes *multiplication*

   diversify becomes *diversification*

2. Ask students, "Why do you think words use linking letters?" There are a variety of possible answers. The best ones focus on how linking letters are needed to help with pronunciation. Try to say *imaginetion, reproducetion,* or *multiplytion*. Linking letters helps to make words easier to pronounce, syllabicate, and spell.

3. Have students brainstorm as many multi-syllable words as they can that end in *tion*. Words from the Spelling Variations activity often contain a number of good examples.

4. Have students select a number of these *-tion* words and highlight the linking letters.

5. Ask students to examine their linking-letter words based on the following questions.

   • What happens to silent *e* in these words?

   • What are the most common linking letters? (Answer: *a* and *i*)

   • Do certain linking letters replace other letters most of the time? (Answer: *i* usually replaces *y* and *a* usually replaces *e*.)

Activity Scoring

This task is best evaluated as simply complete or incomplete because of the heavy emphasis on class discussion and its limited independent work.

Special Needs Considerations

Students with special needs find this activity a little more challenging because of the increased level of verbal instruction. Encourage them to follow along as best they can during the class lesson, and review the concept individually at a later date to ensure comprehension.

Linking Letters Extension: The Linking Letter Quest!

Challenge students to find other linking letters hidden in multisyllable words (e.g., *d* for *s*: *explode/explosion*; *t* for *ss*: *permit/permission*; *b* for *p*: *describe/description*; *c* for *t*: *essence/essential*).

Y Do I Always Get Dropped?

This activity is the first of three that examines the use of *es* when making a word plural. It reviews how words ending in *y* drop this final letter and replace it with *i* before adding the suffix *-es*. Framing this individual plural pattern with others that are similar helps students to create a better understanding of when to use this *es* plural pattern.

Materials

- photocopies of Reproducible 27, *Y Do I Always Get Dropped?* (one for each team)
- dictionaries (one for each team)

Lesson Format

Objective: Students will be able to explain that when *y* is the final letter in a word it is consistently changed to an *i* if a suffix is added.

Procedure:

1. Complete this activity using the general procedures outlined earlier in this chapter (see page 49).

2. At the conclusion of the activity, discuss with the class that there are really only three times when we use *es* instead of *s* when making a word into a plural:

- When words end in *y*, we replace the *y* with an *i*.

- When words end in *f*, we replace the *f* with a *v* (e.g., *calf/calves*).

- When words end in soft sounds (/sh/, /ch/, /ss/, /x/), they have to use *es*; otherwise, it is extremely difficult to hear if the word is plural (e.g., *dishs/dishes*).

Review each of these patterns briefly with your students so they can begin to see these exceptions as belonging to a larger pluralization pattern. Place greater emphasis upon the "replace the *y* with an *i*" pattern presented within Reproducible 27.

Teaching Tips

Emphasize with your students that adding and dropping letters is just another pattern. There are many examples of letters that are added and dropped, such as *e* (e.g., *bake* → *baking*; *imagine* → *imagination*), *y* (e.g., *happy* → *happiness*), and even *f* (e.g., *wolf* → *wolves*). There are also many examples where letters are only added (e.g., *flag* → *flagged*; *begin* → *beginning*). Changing these letter patterns allows the writer to slightly change word meanings so they can be used in a wider range of contexts.

When f Multiplies

When *f* Multiplies reviews how words ending in *f* drop this final consonant and replace it with *v* before adding the suffix *-es*. It is one of the three times that students need to know to use *es* rather than *s* when making a word plural.

Materials

- photocopies of Reproducible 28, When *f* Multiplies (one for each team)
- dictionaries (one for each team)

Advance Preparation

Decide whether this will be completed as an individual or team activity.

Lesson Format

Objective: Students will be able to explain that to make words ending in *f* into a plural, they must replace the *f* with a *v* and add *es*.

Procedure:

1. Discuss with the class the three situations when students need to use *es* instead of *s* when making a plural:

   - In words that end in *f* when we replace the *f* with a *v* (e.g., *calf/calves*).

   - In words that end in soft sounds (/sh/, /ch/, /ss/, /x/). These words have to use *es*; otherwise it is extremely difficult to hear if the word is a plural (e.g., *dishs* versus *dishes*).

   - In words that end in *y* when we replace the *y* with an *i*.

   Review this generalization with your students so they can see that, even with these exceptions, there is a great deal of predictability. Place greater emphasis on the pattern presented in Reproducible 28.

2. Complete the remainder of this activity using the general procedures outlined earlier in this chapter (see page 49). At the conclusion of the activity, ask students to record what they have learned about this word pattern within their Word Patterns page.

Teaching Tips

- Emphasize to your students that although this pattern is a bit of an exception when it comes to making words plural, it is also another example of how frequently the adding and dropping of letters occurs at word endings.
- Connect this add/drop letter pattern with others such as words ending in silent *e* and *y*.

Plurals: s or es?

Despite being quite consistent, the -s/-es suffix pattern for plurals is sometimes a difficult one for students to remember. Most words are made plural by adding s; the -es suffix is only used to form a plural when a word ends in a soft or hissing sound. This soft sound is commonly made by s, x, z, sh, ch.

Materials

• photocopies of Reproducible 29, s or es?

• dictionaries (one for each team)

Lesson Format

Objective: Students will be able to explain why sometimes plural words end in s and other times es.

Procedure:

1. Complete this activity using the general procedures outlined earlier in this chapter (see page 49).

2. At the conclusion of the activity, discuss the three times when we use es instead of s to make a word plural:

• When words end in soft sounds (/sh/, /ch/, /ss/, /x/).

• When words end in y, we replace the y with an i.

• When words end in f, we replace the f with a v (e.g., calf/calves).

Review each of these patterns briefly with your students so they can begin to see these exceptions as belonging to a larger pluralization pattern. Place greater emphasis on the soft-sound pattern presented within Reproducible 29.

Teaching Tips

The -s/-es suffix pattern will make better sense to students if you ask them what would happen to words that end in es if the extra e was not in the suffix. This e separates the last sound in the root word from the suffix (e.g., hisss/hisses and churchs/churches). Without this extra e, it would be difficult to determine whether or not the word was plural.

Patterns Everywhere

Students need to regularly study words and examine language patterns (Butyniec-Thomas & Woloshyn, 1997; Henderson, 1990; Moats, 1995; Wong, 1986). In this activity, students work together to consider the influence of sound, visual cues, and meaning on word spelling.

Advance Preparation

Write sample words on the board or the overhead projector.

Lesson Format

Objective: Students will be able to identify and explain three common letter patterns that occur when suffixes are added to multisyllable words.

Procedure:

1. Write the following suffix-pattern words on the board and ask students to analyze them. Remind them that the spelling of words is influenced by sound, visual cues, and spelling–meaning connections.

   compose/composition

   resign/resignation

   product/production

   mobile/mobility

   locate/location

   receive/reception

2. Ask students to find three common patterns that occur when suffixes are added to the words.

3. Encourage students to initially say the words out loud to check for sound patterns.

4. Ask students to write an explanation of the patterns they find in their notebooks.

Reinforcing the Spelling Strategies

The sample words in this activity provide many opportunities to review Spelling Strategies. At the conclusion of this activity ask students to

- list a number of new words that rhyme with the sample words,

- separate a number of the sample words into syllables,

- make a list of all the smaller words found within a certain number of the longer sample words, and

- list words with spelling–meaning connections for a certain number of the sample words.

Teaching Tips

- For best results, have students work together in teams but individually record what they find within their own notebooks.

- Regularly remind students to consider patterns related to sound, visual cues, and spelling–meaning connections. Encourage them to say the words out loud, to highlight letters that have been added or dropped in each word pair, and to underline the section of each word that has a spelling–meaning connection. These steps provide a systematic thinking structure that helps some students more easily analyze the words.

Special Needs Considerations

Students with special needs find this task challenging because of its open-ended nature and the high-level comparative analysis required. This task asks students to cognitively compare similarities and differences between words and then apply what they have learned to what they know about other common word patterns. To help weaker students, consider pairing them with more capable peers, and encourage them to use the word-analysis strategies presented within the teaching tips section.

Extension: Be a Pattern Detector!

Repeat this process with any pattern that students need additional practice with. All you need to do is decide on the cluster of words to use.

Hidden Connections

This activity highlights how the spelling–meaning connection often occurs in words even when we are not aware of it. Sometimes if the root word has originated from Greek or Latin, this connection is not very clear. It is important to review such connections, however, because these roots can often help us to better predict how a word will be spelled.

Materials

• photocopies of Reproducible 30, Hidden Connections

• dictionaries (one for each student or team)

Advance Preparation

Decide whether this will be completed as an individual or team activity.

Lesson Format

Objective: Students will become more aware of how word history and meaning have an impact on the spelling of many words.

Procedure:

1. Examine a few sample words to highlight the difference between a root, prefix, and suffix.

2. Assign Reproducible 30 and monitor student progress.

3. Collect and mark the reproducibles.

Activity Scoring

Mark this activity out of 5 points. Deduct one-half point for every box that is not completed accurately.

Extensions: Considering Connections

To properly see the connections between Latin and Greek words with spelling–meaning connections, students need regular exposure to this link. The following extensions will help you reinforce spelling–meaning connections.

• A simple sponge activity to practice this is the Expanding Words Activity format. Simply list a Greek or Latin root on the board for students to brainstorm other connected words from. For example, if you list the word *sign*, students could brainstorm connected words such as *signals*, *signature*, *signboard*, or *significance*. The words listed in this assignment, and in Become an Etymologist, will provide a good start. Encourage students to use their dictionaries to find even more connections.

• Another simple sponge activity is to place a Latin or Greek root on the board and ask students to figure out its meaning. Encourage them to use the dictionary to examine all the other words with spelling–meaning connections. Often this helps students to see the connection more clearly.

ed Endings

This activity highlights whether the last letter of a word should be doubled, dropped, or remain unchanged when adding the suffix -*ed*. In general, students should double letters that are preceded by a short vowel and drop the letters *y* or *e* before adding the suffix.

Materials

• photocopies of Reproducible 31, *ed* Endings (one for each student or team)

Advance Preparation

Decide whether this will be completed as an individual or team activity.

Lesson Format

Objective: Students will be able to better explain whether to add or drop letters when adding -*ed* suffixes.

Procedure:

1. Complete this activity using the general procedures outlined earlier in this chapter (see page 49).

2. At the conclusion of the activity, ask students to record on the Word Patterns page of their notebooks what they have learned about this word pattern.

Extension: Dissecting Words

This is a good activity for emphasizing how syllables are often split between twinned letters, and that the placement of syllable breaks is influenced by short and long vowel sounds within the syllables. The sample words in this activity also provide an opportunity to review other spelling strategies. At the conclusion of this activity, ask students to

• list a number of new words that rhyme with the sample words,

• separate a number of the sample words into syllables,

• make a list of all the smaller words found within a number of the longer sample words, and

• list all the words with spelling–meaning connections for a number of the sample words.

Supplementary Activities

Spelling can be taught in more than just isolated lessons. There are numerous ways to extend spelling practice into other curriculum areas. Many of the Pattern Activities and Thinking Activities can be used in content areas. I have used the following instructional strategies successfully in a variety of reading, writing, science, math, and even art assignments. They will help you integrate spelling practice in all subjects.

Redirecting the Question

When students ask how to spell a word, answer the question with a question: "What spelling strategies could you use?" or "What patterns do you see?" Strategic Spelling is only useful to the extent that it becomes part of your daily instructional routine—and students' daily reading and writing. There are many teachable spelling moments that arise during reading and writing activities across the curriculum. Seize some of these opportunities to point out such things as why a letter is doubled (or dropped) and when a suffix is added.

Self-Assessment

Student self-assessment spelling strategies, such as Thoughtful Editing, T-Chart Check, and Pick & Pattern, described in the next chapter, place the responsibility with students for finding and correcting spelling mistakes. Versions of these strategies can be incorporated in almost any reading or writing lesson so students examine language patterns across the curriculum. This allows spelling instruction to be blended into a variety of activities instead of always being an isolated lesson.

Spelling Stories

Spelling Stories is an editing activity that is ideal to use after a holiday or break. Direct students to write one paragraph of about five to seven sentences, with approximately 10 hidden errors. The errors may be in spelling, punctuation, grammar, capitalization, verb tense, paragraph formation, etc. Encourage students to have fun writing the paragraph and to exaggerate some of the things that happen in the story. Once students have completed the paragraph, ask them to rewrite the paragraph on a separate sheet, underlining all the intentional errors and correcting them.

Select a few of the best paragraphs and photocopy them onto an overhead projector transparency. Then challenge the class to see if they are "smart enough" to find all the errors. For the student whose work is chosen, it is always fun to relax and watch the rest of the class work away on their assignment. A good way to introduce this activity is to ask the class to edit one of your own exaggerated paragraphs. Students love trying to trick their classmates!

Writing Spelling Stories on the Computer

Most computers have spelling checkers and thesauruses. Teach your students to use these resources by having them create a spelling story. In this activity, students create a short story on the computer (no more than half a page). When they have finished their story drafts, teach them how to use the spelling checker. After students have corrected their spelling errors, have them underline 10 interesting words in the story. Then ask them to copy and paste their story below the first, creating two identical paragraphs on the same page. Have students replace the 10 underlined words in the second paragraph with other related words from the computer thesaurus. Encourage students to replace the words they have chosen with *more interesting* words. The end result is an assignment containing an original paragraph and a second, improved paragraph that has been edited by students using both the spelling checker and the thesaurus.

Peer Editing

Divide the class into pairs to proofread one another's written work. Ask students to underline or correct a specified number of errors on their partner's paper (5–10 works well). If students cannot find the required number of errors, they must show the assignment to you to see if they have missed any. If you find additional errors, give them a hint but have them keep searching. When all the pairs are finished editing, they sign the top of their partner's assignment to indicate that they have edited the work to the best of their ability.

Pattern Search

After your class has completed a few Thinking Activities, ask them to find specific language patterns in a text unrelated to the spelling lessons. See if students can find some of the language patterns they have been studying. This exercise enriches any lesson that involves reading. Just make it clear to students which patterns they should try to find.

Graphing the Pattern

Graphing language patterns is a cross-curricular link among English, science, math, and computers (graphics). The Thinking Activities provide a number of language patterns that can be compared, graphed, analyzed, and discussed. If your class is having a difficult time with a specific language pattern, consider graphing the *frequency* of the pattern within a selected piece of text. This text could come from a textbook, novel, magazine, or newspaper. You can create graphs to illustrate and compare the frequency with which words within the text

- use prefixes or suffixes;
- use one, two, three, or more syllables;
- drop a letter when adding a suffix;
- add a letter when adding a suffix;
- use long or short vowel sounds;
- use letter combinations that make certain sounds; and
- demonstrate patterns from previous Thinking Activities.

Graphing provides a creative way to illustrate and compare many language patterns. For example, the /k/ sound is made by several letter combinations (*kite, cake, torque, deck,* and *chrome*). In the popular nursery rhyme line "Jack be nimble, Jack be quick, Jack jump over the candle stick," the /k/ sound is represented by three different letter combinations: *ck* five times, *c* once, and *q* once. Even this one line provides an opportunity to review three important language patterns: *ck* is used mainly after a vowel at the end of a word, *c* often makes the /k/ sound when followed by a vowel; and *q* always needs to be spelled with the letter *u.* Graphs provide an alternate method to discuss the frequency and positioning of language patterns within words (e.g., next to vowels or consonants, at the beginning or end of the word). By having students create graphs, you provide them with repeated encounters with the pattern as well as a concrete, visual memory aid. See Figure 8 for a sample graph of word endings in *Mrs. Frisby and the Rats of NIMH* (O'Brien, 1971).

The Art of Spelling

From time to time, consider integrating spelling into art lessons to give students additional practice with a difficult concept in a fun and creative format. Some art–spelling activities are as follows:

- Create posters that demonstrate language patterns (see the Thinking Activity Prefixes and Suffixes Poster).

- Make a collage of cutouts from newspapers and magazines to represent what students think, know, and feel about words or spelling.

- Demonstrate a language pattern through art (e.g., drawing pictures of words that rhyme or are in the same word family, or drawing a series of pictures that illustrate the smallest root word to the largest word form).

- Create a class word wall. After the class completes some of the Thinking Activities, create a mural of all the language patterns they have found. Have each student team take responsibility for representing one language pattern in the mural. Ask them to include an explanation of the pattern, evidence, and artwork. The teams can present their part of the word wall publicly to practice public speaking.

Word Connection

Word Connection develops student awareness of the connections among words. Select a word and have students find an *antonym* (a word that means the opposite) and a *synonym* (a word that

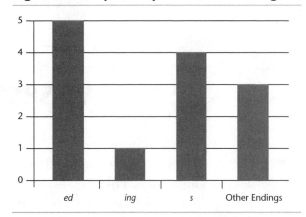

Figure 8. Sample Graph of Word Endings

Word endings were tallied from the novel *Mrs Frisby and the Rats of NIMH* (O'Brien, 1971).

means the same). Then have them write a sentence or two using all three words, as shown:

Word: *fantastic*

Antonym: *average*

Synonym: *exceptional*

Sentence: Marisol is not an average student. She is an exceptional thinker who is fantastic at everything she tries.

You can make the activity more challenging by asking students to list three to five antonyms and synonyms for the word you give. This activity can also be used to teach students how to use a thesaurus.

Conclusion

Chapters 3 through 5 have presented various ideas to develop more independent and confident spellers. Keep in mind, however, that Strategic Spelling is one piece of larger classroom literacy instruction. To maximize student learning, complement Strategic Spelling with significant reading and writing practice. In the next chapter, practical and effective assessment methods are outlined to help you measure student progress.

Assessment

chap·ter 6

Proper assessment is the common thread that runs through all effective, ongoing instruction. It enables you to be responsive to the needs of your students. Assessing student progress in Strategic Spelling is no different from assessing students in other areas. Routine assessment is essential to the effectiveness of the approach.

Traditionally, spelling has been treated as a memory task that is measured by weekly spelling tests. This kind of assessment is assessment *of* learning. It is a black-and-white, evaluative approach that offers little insight into the difficulties students are having.

To make assessment more relevant, educators must place greater emphasis on teacher observations, diagnostic testing, and student self-assessment. Together, these three measures provide useful information about the specific difficulties with which students are struggling. This shift in focus is important because "the best instruction grows out of paying close attention to what children are doing: looking at their spellings, noticing how they come up with spellings, and asking them about spelling" (Sandra Wilde, as cited in Laminack & Wood, 1996, p. x).

There is no ideal method to collect all this spelling information. Students, educators, and learning environments vary too widely for one method to work in all situations (Kosnik, 1998). By combining your professional judgment with best practices, you can determine the assessment methods that work best in your classroom. Sandra Wilde summarizes spelling best practices as four principles:

1. Spelling is evaluated on the basis of natural writing rather than on tests.

2. Spelling is evaluated analytically rather than as merely right or wrong.

3. Spelling is looked at in terms of students' use of strategies rather than in isolation.

4. Educators evaluate spelling as informed professionals rather than as mechanical test scorers. (cited in Laminack & Wood, 1996, pp. 12–13)

I add a fifth principle to this list:

5. Evaluation of spelling must include self-assessment opportunities that allow students to actively analyze their own spelling efforts and develop greater ownership.

Wilde's four spelling-assessment principles provide a great deal of useful evaluative information about assessment of learning. We need to ensure that students are receiving this information in a meaningful way. Involving students in the assessment process broadens assessment so that it is not only assessment *of* learning but also assessment *as* learning (Stiggins, 2002). Self-assessment opportunities complement other assessment methods, fostering more thoughtful and reflective spelling.

In a cluttered curriculum, there is limited time to devote to spelling assessment. In a typical class of 25–30 students, assessment methods need to be relatively quick and easy if educators are going to use them (Ganske, 2000).

With this in mind, the remainder of this chapter examines ways to

- gather spelling information from a variety of sources,

- critically examine student work for error patterns, and

- involve students in the assessment process.

It is a framework that acknowledges that spelling assessment is only useful to the extent that it improves instruction and enhances student learning.

Teacher Observations

My own experiences as a classroom teacher have convinced me that the most important part of spelling assessment occurs informally during daily instruction and paper-marking. It is during instruction and marking that spelling-error patterns become evident. Informal assessment provides valuable information about individual student needs and needs of the entire class.

By spending time with students in writing situations across the curriculum, analyzing and discussing the spelling errors in their work, you gain a great deal of information and take advantage of teachable moments. As you examine student work, highlight

- obvious spelling-error patterns (e.g., over-reliance on phonetic spellings),

- consistently added or omitted letters,

- attempts at difficult words (make sure there are ample attempts),

- self-corrected spelling errors (and attempts at self-correction), and

- use of spelling strategies (correct use and attempts).

When marking student work outside of class time, try to provide at least one piece of spelling/writing feedback per assignment. When you hand back student work, draw attention to the feedback prior to discussing the remainder of the task. Provide adequate wait time for students to read and consider feedback before moving on with the review of the assignment.

One effective method for getting students to consider feedback is the Think–Pair–Share strategy (Lyman, 1981). Ask students to quietly think about the feedback you have given, then tell them to turn to a partner and share the feedback. For significant individual feedback, write on the assignment that you would like the student to see you. This allows you to verbally check that students have read and understood the feedback. Checking for comprehension ensures that students consider your feedback.

Ongoing, incidental assessment has become an important part of my teaching repertoire. It provides a global picture of students' spelling abilities and helps me to focus on *how* students arrive at words. To best use informally gathered information, create a system to quickly record the most important observations (e.g., place sticky notes in student files or create an information sheet for each student). Without such a system, it will be difficult to recall and track what you notice.

Diagnostic Testing

Every formal assessment tool has its limitations; all have a certain degree of measurement error. Add to this the numerous patterns and exceptions of the English language. Then consider that all students have a unique profile of language patterns that they have mastered, understandings that they are developing, and language concepts that they do not fully grasp. When all of these factors are considered together, it is easy to see why spelling progress can only be described as a series of broadly based developmental stages.

In the middle grades, most students are operating in the highest two developmental spelling stages (Syllable Juncture and Derivational Constancy). To determine which stage a student is in, compare the student's spelling errors to the core concepts in each stage. Reproducible 32, Spelling Stages Checklist, lists the main diagnostic features of the spelling stages.

Knowing the developmental spelling stages students are in helps you to focus classroom instruction. This general information needs to be accompanied by specific details about the error patterns and spelling-strategy usage of individual students. You will become aware of many of these spelling tendencies during daily classroom routines. More formal diagnostic testing can help to validate your observations and to highlight unique strengths, weaknesses, and patterns. In my own classroom practice, I have relied heavily on two formal diagnostic measures:

1. an error analysis of written work, and

2. diagnostic spelling tests.

Error Analysis of Written Work

I believe error analysis is the most important spelling diagnostic tool because it quickly measures student spelling competency in a writing context. It is a relatively simple measure to administer, and when used at logical intervals (e.g., at the beginning of the year and at reporting periods), it can provide valuable data. For most students, using more detailed spelling-assessment methods than this is of minimal benefit when you consider the testing time they take (Westwood, 1999).

To begin an error analysis, all you need is an unedited writing sample (a story draft, unedited class assignment, journal entry, or a report draft). My own preference is to ask students to complete a 30-minute in-class writing assignment. This ensures that all students are writing under the same conditions and have had adequate writing time. Be sure to spend some time

discussing possible writing topics before the 30-minute period begins. I have achieved the best results when students have written on topics of their choosing with prewriting time to help them organize their thoughts.

To evaluate the writing assignments, simply read through them and circle any spelling and punctuation errors. This marking can be done very quickly if you restrict your attention to scanning for spelling-type errors and do not read for meaning. Once you have circled all the errors, separate them into categories. The most common spelling errors of middle school students are included in Reproducible 33, Error Analysis. In the Comments column, you can include notes to help you place students' spelling within a greater writing context. Write your observations of students' use of vocabulary, capitalization, punctuation, paragraphs, and writing quantity. Without these comments, some students may appear to be writing well because they have made relatively few spelling mistakes. When examined more globally, however, the reason for the comparatively few spelling errors may be that students were not writing enough or were using simple vocabulary. By including your observations, you create a realistic picture of whether students are truly spelling and writing well.

To complete Reproducible 33, write down students' misspelled words within the appropriate category. Underline the specific error (e.g., _fansy_). Write the correct spelling beside the misspelled one if the word is difficult to decipher out of context (e.g., _forst = forced_, not _forest_). Write check marks beside misspelled words to indicate repeated errors.

Some categories in the assessment overlap. When a student misspells the word _talks_ as _talkes_, he or she has both added a letter and made an affix error. In such situations, choose one category that best reflects the type of error made. In the case of _talkes_, the misspelling is best categorized as an affix error because the student is having difficulty applying plural–suffix patterns.

Diagnostic Spelling Tests

An error analysis is an effective measure of spelling proficiency in written work. It clearly highlights error patterns, but it does not always offer insight into the thinking behind the error patterns. To obtain qualitative information, use the three formalized quizzes included with the Thinking Activities (refer to chapter 4 and the Reproducibles section of this book). When you consider the results of these quizzes in conjunction with your observations and self-assessment data, a clear picture emerges about students' spelling tendencies and progress.

Self-Assessment

Aside from informal observations, self-assessment is the most important part of spelling evaluation. Self-assessment actively involves students in their own learning. It is assessment as learning in the purest sense.

Accurate spelling is hard work. It requires students to self-monitor their written work, reread for accuracy, ask for help, and use a dictionary when necessary. For many students, a lack of these basic skills or a reluctance to use them plays a significant role in their spelling difficulties. It is often hard to know how much of a student's spelling difficulties are the result of language issues, lack of effort, the inability to sustain focus, or working too quickly. By involving students in the assessment process, you encourage them to "buy in," to become more thoughtful and reflective spellers (Tarasoff, 1990).

Three effective ways to involve students in spelling assessment are

1. Thoughtful Editing,

2. T-Chart Check, and

3. Pick & Pattern.

Thoughtful Editing

Thoughtful Editing is an excellent self-assessment strategy because it places the responsibility for finding and correcting spelling mistakes with the students. When editing written work, ask to see some of the assignments at the draft stage. Quickly scan the drafts for errors, and write at the top of the page the number of errors you would like students to find and correct. Do not identify where the errors are. Simply hand back the drafts and ask students to find, underline, and correct their errors. When students return the draft with their corrections, check mark the top of the page to indicate that they can begin working on the final version. The Thoughtful Editing strategy works well because

- students critically reread their own work,

- you can quickly monitor how easy or difficult it is for students to find and correct spelling errors, and

- it is an ideal opportunity to discuss spelling error patterns in a written context with individual students.

The strategy also allows you to choose the number of mistakes each student should find. This flexibility means that you can ask strong students to find more errors than you ask struggling students to find. In general, ask students to find and correct 5–10 errors.

T-Chart Check

T-Chart Check self-assessment can initially be difficult for some students because they are asked to both identify errors and provide patterns and strategies to show how spelling is predictable. Once students are comfortable with the process though, T-Chart Check becomes a powerful self-assessment tool. To help students become more confident, work through a few problem words as a class, then do a few more in small groups. With such a graduated approach, it won't take long for all students to feel confident with the task. For best results, encourage students to regularly refer to Reproducible 1, Spelling Strategies Diagram, and discuss what they notice with their peers.

When students complete an assignment, ask them to create a T-Chart with the headings "Word" and "Pattern." Have them scan the assignment for three to five words that don't look right and write them in the Word column. (If some students legitimately can't find enough misspelled words, ask them to select the words that were most challenging for them to spell.) Have students list the correct spelling of each word below the misspelling and underline the difference between the two versions. For this second step, you may want to consider insisting students use a dictionary if they are not being accurate enough. This visual comparison helps students to more easily complete the next step: writing down the patterns that make the spelling of the word predictable. Students may include visual, sound, or meaning patterns. Students often notice

- rhyming patterns,

- word-in-word patterns,

- spelling–meaning connections,

- common prefixes and suffixes,

- important syllable sounds and breaks, and

- patterns they learned during Thinking Activities.

Sometimes students can explain how they will use patterns to avoid making the same spelling error again, but with all the exceptions and unstressed letters in multisyllable words, it is unrealistic to expect them to be able to explain why every pattern works. However, students should be able to locate and state one or two patterns for each of the words. A great deal of spelling proficiency involves being able to take advantage of common language patterns, so make sure that this is the focus of the T-Chart Check.

Variations on Thoughtful Editing and T-Chart Check

To vary Thoughtful Editing and T-Chart Check, organize them as collaborative activities and occasionally add a metacognitive concluding question. Both self-assessments work well as peer-assessment tasks in which partners follow the steps of Thoughtful Editing or T-Chart Check to find the errors in one another's work. Provide clear expectations about how you want students to correct the errors in their partner's work, and provide time for students to share the corrections with their partners.

Another variation of Thoughtful Editing and T-Chart Check is to ask students to complete a concluding sentence, for example, "One thing I noticed about my spelling (or thinking) today was...." This structured, metacognitive question provides some very interesting information about students' thinking.

Pick & Pattern

Pick & Pattern self-assessment is quicker and simpler to use than Thoughtful Editing and T-Chart Check, but it also generates the least amount of useful spelling information. The strength of Pick & Pattern is that it can be used in almost any reading or writing lesson to get students quickly reflecting on spelling patterns.

At any point during a reading or writing assignment, ask students to find a word that either doesn't look right or is challenging for them. Alternatively, you may select a word for the class. Have students circle the word if it is in their notebooks; if the word is in a textbook, have them point to it. Give students 1 minute to think about what is predictable about the word. Encourage them to refer to Reproducible 1, Spelling Strategies Diagram, and to use the dictionary. Ask students to write down what they notice and then share it with a partner. After all the pairs have shared, select a couple of students to share what they noticed with the class in order to maintain accountability.

Using the Measures in Combination

There are numerous formalized spelling assessments that you can use in conjunction with self-assessments. To locate assessment materials, a useful resource is *Words Their Way* (Bear et al., 2000). This text contains several excellent diagnostic spelling assessments, including the McGuffey Qualitative Inventory of Word Knowledge (which provides a grade-level equivalency) and the Upper Elementary Spelling Inventory (which identifies specific error patterns).

The only true measure of spelling performance is how well students spell in their written work, but formal diagnostic measures that use isolated words do provide useful information. With the limited assessment time in the classroom, however, the majority effort needs to be on spelling in written work.

When assessing spelling progress, consider a range of writing samples, assignments, and more formal diagnostic assessments. Error analysis provides valuable, specific information, but it is still only based on *one* unedited writing sample. Informal observations provide an overall sense of students' spelling abilities, but they are not ideal for systematically detecting a range of error patterns. Self-assessments offer insight into students' thinking processes, but may not be the best method to fully understand the frequency and range of students' specific spelling difficulties because students select the errors to be examined. To achieve a complete picture of student spelling competency, consider all three measures—error analysis, informal observation, self-assessment—together.

con·clu·sion

Teaching students about language patterns is one of the cornerstones of effective teaching. The English language is full of patterns that help us to read and write effectively. Unfortunately, in the hectic race to memorize, assign, test, and discuss exceptions, many spelling programs have obscured some important patterns. In general, educators do not spend enough time training middle school students how to notice language patterns and how to apply effective spelling strategies. More than anything else, spelling instruction in the middle grades needs to focus on patterning, thinking, and strategy usage: "The use of strategies and the knowledge of patterns go hand in hand—they help make English less confusing and provide students with the tools to use when spelling" (Kosnik, 1998, p. 62).

Accurate spelling is the result of complex higher order thinking. It is not the result of systematic word memorization. Good writers gradually learn to spell most words while absorbed in meaningful reading and writing activities. The teacher's role, then, is to highlight the predictability of English and to teach strategies that take advantage of its predictability.

Strategic Spelling offers activities and strategies that revitalize spelling instruction. Its instructional format is not only teacher friendly, interesting for students, and effective, but also it is built on research that indicates the following:

- The human brain is a pattern seeker.

- Most students engage in systematic spelling strategies.

- Good spellers unconsciously use a number of specific strategies.

- Learning is enhanced when students demonstrate an understanding of how something works rather than merely reciting facts.

Strategic Spelling uses these findings as the basis for its engaging and appropriate spelling methodology. Through the use of word sorts, pattern activities, cooperative learning methods, explicit strategy instruction, and a wide variety of cognitively challenging activities, middle school students become consciously aware of *how* to spell better. They learn to view spelling as a puzzle that can be solved rather than as something unpredictable and confusing that must be memorized.

With this book, you will be able to help students notice sound, visual, and meaning patterns in the English language. The Thinking Activities, Pattern Activities, and Supplementary Activities encourage students to become more strategic spellers by teaching them to think about how words are constructed. Spelling begins to make sense to students because they see how concrete strategies and visible patterns can help them become better spellers.

Examining how language patterns, strategy instruction, and critical thinking can be combined to produce superior spelling instruction has helped me to grow immensely as a teacher. It has helped me create and take advantage of many more teachable spelling moments across the curriculum. I hope that you find these ideas, activities, and strategies as useful as I have and that they finally give you an answer to that familiar student question. Now when a student asks how to spell a word, your answer will always be the same: "What patterns do you see? What strategies could you use?"

re·pro·duc·ibles

Spelling Strategies Diagram

Name_____ Date_____

Most times, if a word **looks** or **feels** right, it is!
Still unsure? Choose your strategy!

Different Spellings
Use only when you know a word but are unsure about a letter or two. Write down possible spellings to see what looks and feels right!

Syllables
Works with longer words.
Divide the word into its sound parts.
Remember, every syllable
1. contains a vowel
2. can help you know if there is one or two of a letter in a word

Word-in-Word
Listen for smaller words or word segments inside longer words. These smaller words are often spelled the same!

Spelling–Meaning Connection
Words with similar meanings often have similar spellings.
For example:
crime/criminal
act/action/activity

Rhyme
Works with shorter words and endings of longer words.

Think of words that sound the same and follow the letter pattern.

Correct Spelling
or
Use a Dictionary
(If the word still doesn't look and feel right)

Word Lists for Word Challenge

Long Words (Syllables, Word-in-Word, and Spelling–Meaning Connections)

abracadabra
acknowledgment
albacore
ambassadorial
anthropological
batholith
bibliography
companion
complication
contemporary
continentalism
deduction
discrimination
elasmobranch
electrocardiograph
exhibition
fearsome
forbidden

geomorphological
gobbledygook
grindstone
hydrofoil
ignoramus
indestructible
indignation
inexplicability
insertion
international
intervention
loudspeaker
lubricant
lubrication
medicinal
obligation
photomicrograph
qualification

rebellious
reincarnation
renunciation
southwestwardly
statesmanship
substitutional
swineherd
temperamental
terrorization
thermodynamics
tractability
trustworthy
uninhabited
unintelligible
unrestrained
zooplankton

Short Words (Rhyme)

abate
abode
abstain
abut
amble
anode
aspire
astute
bovine
cleave
compare
dib
dike
din
dote
drool
eclair
educe

fen
fetlock
geeky
girt
glee
glib
glint
grosbeak
henbane
hind
incline
inflate
jute
ketch
lark
luff
lumbar
lute

mangle
muck
mung (bean)
pew
preen
quaint
quince
scattle
shank
simper
skedaddle
trestle
whoop
yawl
yore
zeal

Prove the Pattern

Name_____ Date_____

<table>
<tr>
<td>

Prove the Pattern

1. Predicted spelling _____

_____

2. Syllables _____

_____

3. Four words that rhyme _____

_____

_____

4. Words inside the word _____

_____

_____

5. Main root word_____

_____

6. Words connected by meaning_____

_____

7. Actual spelling _____

_____

</td>
<td>

Prove the Pattern

1. Predicted spelling _____

_____

2. Syllables _____

_____

3. Four words that rhyme _____

_____

_____

4. Words inside the word_____

_____

_____

5. Main root word_____

_____

6. Words connected by meaning_____

_____

7. Actual spelling _____

_____

</td>
</tr>
</table>

Picking Out Patterns Table

Name_____ Date_____

Word				Spelling Strategies

Starter Words for Scattered Syllables

Scattered Syllables Starter Words

ambassador = ma • sba • as • dor

anaconda = na • a • nco • ad

congratulations = noc • rgta • u • la • ionts

conversation = nco • rev • as • nito

correspond = cro • re • nposd

dependable = ed • nepd • aleb

dramatize = rad • am • ztie

expression = xe • srep • nsoi

hospitality = soh • ip • lta • i • yt

incompatible = in • cmo • tpa • i • ble

probably = ropb • a • byl

subcontractor = bsu • onc • crat • rot

tomorrow = to • rom • wro

unconventional = nu • cno • nve • ntoi • la

underpopulated = nu • rde • ppo • u • tal • de

Tough Guys (mixed by letter and syllable order)

biodegradable = blea • ibo • ed • drag

entertainment = tenm • ne • nati • ret

inexpensive = xe • vesi • ni • npe

prescription = nito • cpsir • erp

Starter Words for Rhyme Time and Word Association

bag	lame	ride
bank	late	rip
blink	line	roll
boil	luck	sack
bold	made	sad
bone	make	sing
bug	mat	sock
dash	mill	sore
day	name	sun
deal	nest	sunk
fail	night	thin
fall	nut	top
feet	oak	tow
flip	pit	tray
hand	poke	went
ice	rain	whine
jump	ran	

Starter Words for Word Detective

abnormalism	lamebrain
antivaccinationism	overcareful
aqueduct	plowboy
artless	sunshade
catbird	tailgate
counterculturalism	telespectroscope
electromagnetism	tenderhearted
hardpan	thumbscrew
hornbook	toastmaster
inexhaustibility	

Match the Meaning Worksheet

Name _____ Date _____

Match the Meaning

1. Beginning Word _____

2. Connected Word _____

3. How are their meanings the same?
_____
_____
_____

4. How are their meanings slightly different?
_____
_____
_____

Match the Meaning

1. Beginning Word _____

2. Connected Word _____

3. How are their meanings the same?
_____
_____
_____

4. How are their meanings slightly different?
_____
_____
_____

Match the Meaning

1. Beginning Word _____

2. Connected Word _____

3. How are their meanings the same?
_____
_____
_____

4. How are their meanings slightly different?
_____
_____
_____

How Short and Long Get Along

Name_____ Date_____

Short and long vowel sounds give us a lot of clues about how to spell words. They hold the key to many important spelling patterns.

Long vowels say their own name, as in *pay* or *name*.

Short vowels do not say their own name and are much more brief, as in *ham* and *jam*.

1. In the table below, indicate whether the letter patterns make a long or short vowel sound, and then provide three examples to prove you are right.

Letters	Short or Long Vowel Sound?	Evidence
-ick	short	brick, kick, stick
-ide		
-ight		
-ump		
-ock		
-ine		
-ain		
-oke		
-unk		
-ail		
-ill		
-ip		
-ash		
-ug		
-ake		
-eed		
-ack		
-in		
-am		

2. A common letter pattern that occurs with short vowel sounds is: _____

3. A common letter pattern that occurs with long vowel sounds is: _____

The Magic e

Name_____ Date_____

Vowels make a variety of sounds. Most of the time these sounds are described as either long or short vowel sounds.

Long vowels say their own name, as in *cane, mine, rode, feed,* and *moan.*

Short vowel sounds make a short sound, as in *cat, hit, hurt, hot,* and *can.*

1. Categorize the following words according to their middle vowel sounds. Write the words that have a short vowel sound in the first column and the words that have a long vowel sound in the second column.

   *car, care, bit, bite, not, note, hit, mice, far, fare
   can, cane, mop, mole, spit, fin, fine, rod, rode
   hut, flute, cap, cape, fir, fire, cup, tune, rot, rote*

Short Vowel Sounds   Long Vowel Sounds

_____   _____

_____   _____

_____   _____

_____   _____

_____   _____

_____   _____

_____   _____

2. What letter patterns do you notice in words that have long vowel sounds?

_____

_____

3. Why is this activity called The Magic *e?*

_____

_____

4. On the back of this sheet, create two columns: one for long vowels and one for short vowels. Then list a word for each vowel sound (long and short) for every vowel (*a, e, i, o,* and *u*); for example, *mate* and *hat* for the long and short sounds of *a.*

Create a Language

A•bish: A pain you get when you're not expecting it. (For example, "Ouch, I just got a bad abish.")

Abished, Abishing

Cra•li•tious: To end up somewhere unexpectedly without knowing how you got there. (For example, "How did I get here? This is very cralitious.")

Craled, Craling

Frook: To bang into something when you're not paying attention. (For example, Bang! "Ouch, I frooked.")

Frooked, Frooking

by Chris Rosenau

When Two Vowels Go Walking

Name_____ Date_____

Words can be broken into sound parts. These "sound parts" are called syllables.
The word *spoken* has two syllables: spo•ken.
The word *syllable* has three syllables: syl•la•ble.

1. Brainstorm and list _____ single-syllable words that have two vowels written together; for example, *wait* and *steam* both have two vowels together (*ai* and *ea*) and both are one syllable.

   _____

   _____

2. Choose ___ of the words you listed above and find them in the dictionary. Write these words using the following pattern:

   example: a. steam p. 437 - stem, stam

   a._____ p._____ - _____,_____   b. _____ p._____ - _____,_____

   c._____ p._____ - _____,_____   d. _____ p._____ - _____,_____

   e._____ p._____ - _____,_____   f. _____ p._____ - _____,_____

3. Say the words from number 2 out loud. Compare the sound of vowels that are **together** to the sound of vowels that are **apart**.

4. Find a pattern in the words for vowels that are **together** and vowels that are **apart**. Use this information to complete the verse:

   When two vowels go walking, the . . .

   _____

   _____

5. Using your dictionary, find _____ multisyllable words that contain **two** vowels together and write them below.

   _____

6. Does the pattern you wrote down in number 4 always work with multisyllable words? Circle the best answer:

   Never   **Sometimes**   **Most times**   **Always**

Is It ei or ie?

Name_____ Date_____

1. Sort the following words into three columns based on the sounds the vowels make. Say each word out loud as you place it into a column.

/a/ sound	/e/ sound	/i/ sound
_____	_____	_____
_____	_____	_____
_____	_____	_____
_____	_____	_____
_____	_____	_____
_____	_____	_____
_____	_____	_____
_____	_____	_____

achieve   eight   pie   shriek

belief   feisty   piece   thief

brief   field   receive   tie

die   freight   relief   weight

diet   lie   retrieve

2. When you are not sure whether a word is spelled with *ei* or *ie*, what would be your best guess? Why? _____

_____

3. Write a spelling rule to explain when to use the vowel patterns *ie* and *ei* in most situations. *Hint*: Do not write down the rule "*i* before *e* except after *c*." Look for a pattern.

_____

_____

_____

_____

Vowel Variations

Name_____   Date_____

1. Cut out the words.

2. Categorize them according to vowel sound.

3. Create a heading for each category based on the vowel sound.

4. Explain to your teacher why the categories you have chosen make sense.

5. Write the categories in marker across the top of the sheet of construction paper. Write the names of the team members on the back.

6. Glue the words under their category headings, leaving one inch across the bottom.

7. In this one-inch bottom space, write what you have noticed about the vowels and their sounds.

air	dawn	leave
ale	fair	made
ask	great	measure
boat	hand	paw
brass	have	ranch
call	heart	ray
cap	jacket	talk
craft	laugh	water
cram	learn	wear

Fat or Skinny CaKe?

Name_____ Date_____

1. Brainstorm and list _____ words that start with a /k/ sound, for example *cake*, *kite*, and *cup*.

_____

_____

_____

_____

2. Choose _____ words from your list and divide them into two equal columns:

Words beginning with *c*   Words beginning with *k*

_____ _____   _____ _____

_____ _____   _____ _____

_____ _____   _____ _____

_____ _____   _____ _____

_____ _____   _____ _____

_____ _____   _____ _____

_____ _____   _____ _____

3. Compare the vowels used in the words above. Find the pattern that can help you know when to use either *c* or *k* at the beginning of words. *Hint*: Look to vowels for help! Describe the pattern:

_____

_____

_____

_____

4. Write down one *other* letter that makes a /k/ sound at the beginning of a word and give an example of a word that uses it:

Letter: _____ Word: _____

Crack the Code

1. List _____ words which end in a /k/ sound, such as *crack* and *bank*.
   Use the dictionary to check the spelling of any confusing words.

   k endings   *ck* endings

   _____   _____

   _____   _____

   _____   _____

   _____   _____

   _____   _____

   _____   _____

2. Compare the kinds of letters that come before the *k* and *ck* endings in the words listed above.
   What pattern(s) do you notice that can help you know when to use *ck* or *k* at the end of most
   words?

   _____

   _____

   _____

   _____

3. How is this pattern different from the pattern you recently learned for words beginning with the
   /k/ sound? *Hint*: Review what you wrote about the Fat or Skinny CaKe rule!

   _____

   _____

   _____

   _____

4. There are five common letters, or combinations of letters, that make the /k/ sound in words. Some
   words use *k* as in *king* or *ck* as in *rock*. Find three other ways that you can make the /k/ sound.

   1.   2.   3.

Thinking Activity Quiz 1

Name_____ Date_____

1. What effect does a silent *e* have when placed at the end of a short word?

   _____

   Examples: a._____   b._____

2. How are dictionary definitions designed to be predictable?

   _____

   _____

3. What spelling pattern can help you to know whether to use a *c* or *k* in a word that begins with a /k/ sound? (Example: *car* or *kick*)

   _____

   _____

   List three examples of the pattern:
   Examples: a._____   b._____   c._____

4. Explain the spelling pattern demonstrated in the following words:
   boat, treat, wait, fail, coat, meat, mail, cheat

   _____

   _____

5. Why is it important to consider meaning when you are spelling a difficult word?

   _____

   _____

6. Are more words spelled with the vowel combination *ei* or *ie*?

   _____

7. What pattern can help you decide whether to use *ei* or *ie* in a word?

   _____

   _____

8. Why is it helpful to listen for small words within long ones?

   _____

   _____

9. Name three strategies that can help you to spell *long* words:
   a._____   b._____   c._____

10. Name two strategies that can help you to spell *short* words:
    a._____   b._____

Homonym Poem

Name_____   Date_____

Eye halve a spelling chequer   _____

It came with my pea sea   _____

It plainly marks four my revue   _____

Miss steaks eye kin knot sea.   _____

Eye strike a key and type a word   _____

And weight four it two say   _____

Weather eye am wrong oar write   _____

It shows me strait a weigh.   _____

As soon as a mist ache is maid   _____

It nose bee fore two long   _____

And eye can put the error rite   _____

Its rare lea ever wrong.   _____

Eye have run this poem threw it   _____

I am shore your pleased two no   _____

Its letter perfect awl the weigh   _____

My chequer tolled me sew.   _____

Author Unknown

Strategic Spelling: Moving Beyond Word Memorization in the Middle Grades by Jonathan P. Wheatley.
Copyright 2005 by the International Reading Association. May be copied for classroom use.

Homonym Headaches

Name_____ Date_____

Homonyms are words that sound the same, are spelled differently, and have different meanings (for example, *their*, *there*, and *they're*).

1. List ___ pairs of homonyms below.

_____   _____   _____

_____   _____   _____

_____   _____   _____

_____   _____   _____

_____   _____   _____

_____   _____   _____

_____   _____   _____

2. Choose ___ pairs of hard-to-remember homonyms from the list you made and underline the difference in their spellings.

3. Find a clue in the definition of the words to help you remember the right spelling for each word in the pairs; for example, you can remember that the number 4 is spelled *four* (not *for*) because it contains 4 letters. Similarly, one way to remember the correct homonym for writing words is to recall that *writing* begins with the same letter as *word*.

4. Write each of the homonym pairs with their spelling clues below to help you remember the spelling of the words and their meanings.

_____

_____

_____

_____

5. What are the three things a word must have to be a homonym?

1. _____

2. _____

3. _____

Ch, tch, cha!

1. Brainstorm and list _____ words that end with the /ch/ sound, such as *witch* and *such*.

_____

_____

_____

2. Rewrite ___ of these words on two separate lists depending on whether they end in *ch* or *tch*.
   (If you are not sure how to spell a word, look it up in the dictionary.)

   tch endings   *ch* endings

   _____   _____

   _____   _____

   _____   _____

   _____   _____

   _____   _____

   _____   _____

   _____   _____

3. Use the lists above to find a pattern that explains when words use *ch* or *tch* at the end of a word.
   Write a spelling rule to explain this pattern. *Hint*: Look at the letters before the /ch/ sound!

   _____

   _____

   _____

4. How is this pattern similar to the pattern we learned for words that end in *k* or *ck* (e.g., *sank, park, drink* versus *kick, smack, back*)?

   _____

   _____

   _____

Predictable Patterns

Name_____ Date_____

1. Brainstorm and list ___ words that end with the /shun/ sound. Then place them in the categories below. Check the spelling of the words in the dictionary if necessary.

tion Endings	*sion* Endings	Other Endings
_____	_____	_____
_____	_____	_____
_____	_____	_____
_____	_____	_____
_____	_____	_____

2. What letter pattern is found most often at the end of words using the /shun/ sound?

_____

3. If you were not sure of the spelling of a word ending in the /shun/ sound, what would be your best guess? Why?

_____

_____

_____

4. Brainstorm and list ___ words that end in either *able* or *ible*. Place them in the categories below. Check the spelling of any difficult words in the dictionary.

-able	*-ible*
_____	_____
_____	_____
_____	_____
_____	_____
_____	_____

5. If you didn't know whether a word ended with *able* or *ible*, what would be your best guess? Why?

_____

_____

6. Look closely at the root words above. What pattern do you notice?

_____

_____

_____

Y Endings Are Easy!

Name_____ Date_____

1. Read the following words out loud:
   crazily, sadly, critically, sneakily, frankly, magically, logically, safely, smoothly, dusty, scientifically, friskily, directly, proudly, surgically

2. What letter pattern(s) do you notice at the end of all of the words?

   _____

   _____

3. What do you notice about the sound at the end of all of the words?

   _____

   _____

4. Sort the words listed into two categories:

   -ly   *-ally*

   _____   _____

   _____   _____

   _____   _____

   _____   _____

   _____   _____

5. How do you know whether to spell a word with *ly* or *ally*?
   Hint: Look for letter patterns and sound patterns.

   _____

   _____

6. Choose _____ words from the list. For each one you choose, write down a related word (one that has a spelling–meaning connection).

   _____   _____

   _____   _____

   _____   _____

   _____   _____

   _____   _____

The Vanishing e

1. Brainstorm and list _____ words that end in *e* (e.g., *make* and *flame*).

_____

_____

_____

2. Find five of these words in the dictionary. List them and the dictionary page numbers below in the spaces provided under question 3.

3. Now list the spelling of the words with the added suffixes *-ed, -ing,* and *-s.* If one of these suffixes doesn't make sense, find another one that does.

Root word	Dictionary page	Word + 3 suffixes
flame	p. 387	flamed, flaming, flames
_____	_____	_____
_____	_____	_____
_____	_____	_____
_____	_____	_____
_____	_____	_____
_____	_____	_____

4. What happens to most words ending in *e* when a suffix is added? Create a spelling rule to describe the pattern.

_____

_____

_____

5. Does the rule work with multisyllable words (e.g., *realize* and *hypothesize*)? Support your answer with evidence.

_____

_____

_____

Become an Etymologist

Etymology is the study of word origins. Researchers who search for the origins of words are called etymologists. Some of our most common prefixes are based on Greek or Latin roots. Look up these Greek and Latin word roots in the dictionary to find some words that use these prefixes today. List at least two words for each prefix in the space provided.

Prefixes	English Meaning	Words Connected By Meaning
sub-	under	
anti-	against	
mono-	one	
dict-	to say	
com-	together	
quadra-	four	
pre-	before	
scrib-	to write	
inter-	between	
post-	after	
fore-	before	
intra-	within	
sign-	mark	
tele-	distant	
photo-	light	
bi-	two	
therm-	heat	
astr-	star	
tri-	three	
super-	over, greater	

What are two things this activity teaches you about words?

1. _____

_____

2. _____

_____

ing Endings

1. Brainstorm and list _____ words that end in *ing*, such as *putting*, *walking*, or *baking*.

_____

_____

_____

_____

2. Separate the above words into two sections. In one section, list all words where the last letter before the *ing* was doubled. In the other section, list all remaining words. If you are unsure of the spelling, check in the dictionary.

Last letter before *ing* is doubled

rebel/rebelling _____

_____

_____

_____

_____

_____

_____

_____

All other words ending in *ing*

face/facing, wink/winking _____

_____

_____

_____

_____

_____

_____

_____

3. How do you know when to double the last letter when adding *ing*? *Hint*: Look at the vowels.

_____

_____

_____

_____

Spelling Variations

Name_____   Date_____

our versus *or*	*s* versus *z*	*re* versus *er*	Other Patterns

Do you think these spelling differences between Canada and the United States will be the same in the future? Explain your answer.

_____

_____

Thinking Activity Quiz 2

Name_____ Date_____

1. What is the most common pattern for words ending in the /shun/ sound?
   _____
   _____

2. What is the difference between a prefix and a suffix?
   _____
   _____

3. List two prefixes and two suffixes.
   Prefixes: _____ _____ Suffixes: _____ _____

4. What spelling pattern is demonstrated at the ends of the following words?
   happy, silly, crazy, nutty, picky, sloppy
   _____
   _____

5. Write down three words that end in *tch* and *ch*.
   -*tch*: _____ _____ _____
   -*ch*: _____ _____ _____

6. How can the letter before *tch* or *ch* help you to know which ending to use?
   _____
   _____

7. What three things does a word need in order to be considered a homonym?
   a. _____
   b. _____
   c. _____

8. The /k/ sound is usually spelled either *ck* or *k*. Some words with these spelling patterns are *chicken, cork, dock, prank, talk, cackle, pick,* and *fork*. What useful pattern indicates whether to use *ck* or *k*?
   _____
   _____

9. When you add the suffix -*ing* to a word, what pattern helps you know whether or not to double the last letter before you add *ing*? (Example: *can* becomes *canning*.)
   _____
   _____

10. When you add a suffix to a word that ends in *e*, what do you need to do?
    _____
    _____

11. What is the spelling–meaning connection? Why is it important to know when you are spelling long words?
    _____
    _____

12. When breaking words into syllables, what two important patterns can help you spell?
    Hint: Think about the Spelling Strategies Diagram.
    _____
    _____

You're the Judge

Name_____ Date_____

The Case: Mission Impossible
The Doubling brothers have claimed that letters in multisyllable words only double when found after a long vowel sound. They want to get rich by making the schools buy new books printed using this rule in them! As the judge, your job is to decide if their pattern works.

1. Evidence
List _____ multisyllable words containing letters that have been doubled (e.g., *billet, rebelled*).

_____

_____

_____

_____

2. Separate the Facts
Examine the words you listed and underline the vowel *before* the doubled letters in each one. Are the vowels short or long? *Hint:* Long vowels say their own name.

_____

List any letters that are doubled more often.

_____

_____

_____

3. The Judgment
Are the Doubling brothers right or wrong? Should we be making textbooks so that letters *only* double after long vowel sounds? Explain your answer.

_____

_____

_____

_____

Y Do I Always Get Dropped?

Name_____ Date_____

1. Brainstorm and list ___ words ending in *y*, such as *crazy* or *family*.

_____

_____

_____

2. What sound pattern do most multisyllable words ending in *y* have in common?

_____

_____

_____

3. Choose _____ of the words from your list and look them up in the dictionary. List the spelling of these words with suffixes such as *-s, -er,* and *-est. Hint*: Not all words will have every ending.

Root word	-s	-er	-est	Other		
_____	_____	_____	_____	_____	_____	_____
_____	_____	_____	_____	_____	_____	_____
_____	_____	_____	_____	_____	_____	_____
_____	_____	_____	_____	_____	_____	_____
_____	_____	_____	_____	_____	_____	_____

4. What happens to words ending in *y* when a suffix is added? Find and describe a pattern.

_____

_____

_____

When f Multiplies

Name_____ Date_____

1. Brainstorm _____ words that end with f, such as *leaf* and *wolf*.

_____

_____

_____

2. Choose at least _____ of these words and write them in the first column below. Find out how to write them as plural words. Write the plural words and the dictionary page in the columns below.

wolf/wolves_____   p. 468   _____   p._____

_____   p._____   _____   p._____

_____   p._____   _____   p._____

_____   p._____   _____   p._____

_____   p._____   _____   p._____

_____   p._____   _____   p._____

_____   p._____   _____   p._____

3. What happens to words ending in *f* when they become plural? Describe the spelling pattern:

_____

_____

_____

4. What other words add or remove letters when changing from a singular to plural? *Hint:* Think about recent spelling activities.

_____

_____

_____

s or es?

1. Brainstorm _____ plural words that end in *s* and *es*.

   s   *es*

   _____   _____

   _____   _____

   _____   _____

   _____   _____

   _____   _____

   _____   _____

   _____   _____

2. Choose ____ *es* ending words from the list above. Use your dictionary to find the root word, suffix (separately), and dictionary page number.

   dish/dishes_____   p. _229_   _____   p._____

   _____   p._____   _____   p._____

   _____   p._____   _____   p._____

   _____   p._____   _____   p._____

   _____   p._____   _____   p._____

   _____   p._____   _____   p._____

   _____   p._____   _____   p._____

3. There are five common letter patterns at the end of words that cause *es* to be used when making a word plural (e.g., *ss* as in *hiss*). Try to list all five!

   _____   _____   _____   _____   _____

4. What letter pattern(s) can help you to know when to use *s* or *es* when making a word plural?

   _____

   _____

   _____

Hidden Connections

Name_____ Date_____

The **root** is the main part of a word, the part that gives it meaning. Some root words are easily visible. For example, *can* is the root of *cannery* and *log* is the root of *logger*. Other root words are less obvious because they are based on words from another language. The table that follows lists some Greek and Latin roots and their English meanings. Look up the Greek and Latin roots in the dictionary to find words that include the root and are connected by meaning. List the related words you find in the last column.

Latin Roots	English Meaning	Words Connected By Meaning
dent	tooth	
aud	hear	
liber	free	
aqua	water	
grat	please	
man	hand	
mar	sea	
mem	mind	
min	small	
sens	feel	
terr	land	
vac	empty	
sign	mark	
bio	life	
cycl	circle	
geo	earth	
gram	written	
hydr	water	
mech	machine	
phon	sound	
ast	star	
chron	time	
opt	eye	

ed Endings

To change most words in the English language into the past tense, you just add the suffix -ed. Some words are special, however—a few of these have been listed below.

trip, walk, kick, supply, bat, study, mine, print, spit, stop, film, blame, develop, identify, reply, sin, play, flip

1. Divide the above words into three equal groups based on what happens at the end of the words when *ed* is added. Use a dictionary to check any difficult spellings.

Double the last letter	Drop or add letters	Just add the *-ed*
_____	_____	_____
_____	_____	_____
_____	_____	_____
_____	_____	_____
_____	_____	_____

2. When the suffix *-ed* is added, what letters are most often dropped?

_____

3. Find a pattern that predicts when the last letter in a word will be doubled if *ed* is added. *Hint*: Listen to the vowel sounds for help.

_____

_____

4. Would this pattern change if the suffix was *-ing* rather than *-ed*?

Yes   No

Explain your answer.

_____

_____

_____

Thinking Activity Quiz 3

Name_____ Date_____

1. Give one example of a word that *ends* with the following letters.

   z: _____ s: _____ sh: _____ ch: _____

   What happens to words that end in these letters when they become plural?

   _____

   _____

2. What do you need to remember when adding suffixes to words that end with *y*?

   _____

   _____

3. What happens to the following words when they become plural? How is this different from what happens to most other plural words?

   wolf   *leaf*   *calf*   *thief*

   _____

   _____

4. Why is it helpful to know the meaning a word when you are spelling it?

   _____

   _____

5. What pattern can help you know whether or not to double the last letter when you are adding a suffix? (Example: *spin* becomes *spinned*.)

   _____

   _____

6. Add *tion* to the end of the following words.

   multiply + tion = _____

   imagine + tion = _____

   summary + tion = _____

   produce + tion = _____

   What useful patterns do you notice in these linking letters?

   _____

   _____

7. Name three strategies that can help you spell *long* words.

   a. _____ b. _____ c. _____

8. Name two strategies that can help you spell *short* words.

   a. _____ b. _____

9. Name two patterns that occur in the middle of syllables that can help you spell. *Hint:* Think about the Spelling Strategies Diagram.

   _____

   _____

10. How have Greek and Latin influenced English? How does being aware of these influences help you spell?

    _____

    _____

    _____

Spelling Stages Checklist

Name_____ Date_____

Students are in the Derivational Constancy Stage when	Yes	Sometimes	No
1. They spell most commonly used multisyllable words correctly.			
2. Their omissions/substitutions tend to be limited to a letter or two and usually make sense (e.g., *compesition/composition, perdictible/predictable*).			
3. They more consistently notice spelling–meaning connections among words. They are tricked less often by vowels or consonants that sound different in related words (e.g., *resign/resignation, oppose/opposition, crime/criminal*).			
Students are in the Syllable Juncture Stage when	**Yes**	**Sometimes**	**No**
1. They read and spell most single-syllable words quickly and accurately.			
2. They are still learning to accurately combine a range of prefixes and suffixes with root words.			
3. They are still learning to consistently double letters (e.g., *trap/trapped, swim/swimming, tennis, manner*).			
4. They are still learning to consistently drop letters (such as the silent *e*) when adding suffixes (e.g., *wave/waving, silly/silliness, multiply/multiplication*).			
5. They are still learning to consistently spell homonyms correctly.			
Students are in the Within Word Pattern Stage when	**Yes**	**Sometimes**	**No**
1. They spell most single-syllable words based on phonetic, sound-based patterns.			
2. They are still learning to consistently spell silent-*e* words correctly.			
3. They are using but are still confusing some consonant blends and vowel digraphs. *Note:* A digraph is two letters that combine to make a new sound (e.g., *s* + *h* = /sh/, *t* + *h* = /th/, *e* + *a* = /ea/).			

Error Analysis

Class: _____ Date: _____

Student Name	Omitted letters (*beutiful* versus *beautiful*)	Additional letters (*hates* versus *hats*)	Substitution of vowels or consonants (*fansy* versus *fancy*)	Transposition of letters (*governmnet* versus *government*)	Homonym Errors (*dear* versus *deer*)	Single/double letter errors (*necesary* versus *necessary*)	Affix errors (*ed, ing, y & i, s & es, ly & lly*)	COMMENTS: written quantity, vocabulary complexity, capitals, punctuation, and paragraphs

ref·er·ences

Adams, M.J. (1990). *Beginning to read: Thinking and learning about print*. Cambridge, MA: The MIT Press.

Anderson, K. (1985). The development of spelling ability and linguistic strategies. *The Reading Teacher, 39*, 140–147.

Askew, M., & Wiliam, D. (1995). Effective questioning can raise achievement. In M. Askew & D. Wiliam, *Recent research in mathematics education 5–16* (OFSTED Reviews of Research, pp. 15–16). London: HMSO. Retrieved December 27, 2004, from http://www.standards.dfes.gov.uk/numeracy/prof_dev/self_study/effectiveteaching/14699/?leaf=0

Bear, D., Invernizzi, M., Templeton, S., & Johnston, F. (2000). *Words their way: Word study for phonics, vocabulary, and spelling instruction*. Upper Saddle River, NJ: Prentice Hall.

Bouffler, C. (1997). They don't teach spelling any more—or do they? *Australian Journal of Language Arts and Literacy, 20*(2), 140–147.

Buchanan, E. (1989). *Spelling for whole language classrooms*. Winnipeg, MN: Whole Language Associates.

Butyniec-Thomas, J., & Woloshyn, V.E. (1997). The effects of explicit-strategy and whole language instruction on students' spelling ability. *The Journal of Experimental Education, 65*, 293–301.

Caine, G., & Caine, R. (1997). *Education: On the edge of possibility*. Alexandria, VA: Association for Supervision and Curriculum Development.

Clark, D.B., & Uhry, J.K. (1995). *Dyslexia: Theory and practice of remedial instruction*. Baltimore: New York Press.

Clymer, T. (1963). The utility of phonic generalizations in the primary grades. *The Reading Teacher, 16*, 252–258.

Coltheart, V., & Leahy, J. (1996). Procedures used by beginning and skilled readers to read unfamiliar letter strings. *Australian Journal of Psychology, 48*(3), 124–129.

Cunningham, P.M. (1998). The multisyllabic word dilemma: Helping students build meaning, spell, and read "big" words. *Reading and Writing Quarterly, 14*(2), 189–218.

Cunningham, P.M. (2000). *Systematic sequential phonics they use*. Greensboro, NC: Carson-Dellosa.

Curtiss, H., & Dolch, E. (1939). Do spelling-books teach spelling? *The Elementary School Journal, 39*, 584–592.

Ehri, L.C. (1989). Development of spelling knowledge and its role in reading acquisition and reading disabilities. *Journal of Learning Disabilities, 22*, 356–370.

Fulk, B.M., & Stormont-Spurgin, M. (1995). Spelling interventions for students with disabilities: A review. *The Journal of Special Education, 28*(4), 488–513.

Gable, R.A., Hendrickson, J.M., & Meeks, J.W. (1988). Assessing spelling errors of special needs students. *The Reading Teacher, 42*, 112–117.

Ganske, K. (2000). *Word journeys: Assessment-guided phonics, spelling, and vocabulary instruction*. New York: Guilford.

Geekie, P., Cambourne, B., & Fitzsimmons, P. (1999). *Understanding literacy development*. Oakhill, UK: Trentham.

Gentry, R. (1982). An analysis of developmental spelling in GNYS AT WRK. *The Reading Teacher, 36*, 192–200.

Gentry, R. (1987). *Spel is a four letter word*. Richmond Hill, Ontario, Canada: Scholastic.

Gentry, R., & Gillet, J.W. (1993). *Teaching kids to spell*. Portsmouth, NH: Heinemann.

Gerber, M.M. (1982). *Effects of self-monitoring on spelling performance of learning disabled and normally achieving students*. Santa Barbara: University of California, Santa Barbara.

Goswami, U. (1992). Annotation: Phonological factors in spelling development. *Journal of Child Psychology and Psychiatry, 33*(6), 967–975.

Graham, S., & Harris, K. (1994). Implications of constructivism for teaching writing to students with special needs. *Journal of Special Education, 28*(3), 275–289.

Graham, S., & Miller, L. (1979). Spelling research and practice: A unified approach. *Focus on Exceptional Children, 12*(2), 1–16.

Gunning, T. (1995). Word building: A strategic approach to the teaching of phonics. *The Reading Teacher, 48*, 484–487.

Hanna, P., Hanna, J., Hodges, R., & Rudorf, E. (1966). *Phoneme–grapheme correspondences as cues to spelling improvement*. Washington, DC: U.S. Government Printing Office.

Hardy, M., Stennett, R.G., & Smythe, P.C. (1973). Word attack: How do they "figure them out"? *Elementary English, 50*, 99–102.

Henderson, E.H. (1990). *Teaching spelling*. Boston: Houghton Mifflin.

Henderson, E.H., & Beers, J. (1980). *Developmental and cognitive aspects of learning to spell: A reflection of word knowledge*. Newark, DE: International Reading Association.

Henderson, E.H., & Templeton, S. (1986). A developmental perspective of formal spelling instruction through alphabet, pattern, and meaning. *The Elementary School Journal, 86*(3), 305–316.

Honig, B. (1997, September). Reading the right way: What research and best practices say about eliminating failure among beginning readers. *School Administrator, 8*(54). Retrieved December 20, 2004, from http://www.aasa.org/publications/sa/1997_09/honig.htm

Hughes, J. (1966). The myth of the spelling list. *National Elementary Principal, 46*, 53–54.

Johnson, D.W., & Johnson, R.T. (1987). *Learning together and alone* (2nd ed.). Englewood Cliffs, NJ: Prentice Hall.

Kagan, S. (1990). *Cooperative learning: Resources for teachers*. San Juan Capistrano, CA: Resources for Teachers.

Kosnik, C. (1998). *Spelling: In a balanced literacy program*. Scarborough, Ontario, Canada: International Thompson Publishing.

Krashen, S. (1989). We acquire vocabulary and spelling by reading: Additional evidence for the input hypothesis. *The Modern Language Journal, 73*, 440–460.

Laminack, L., & Wood, K. (1996). *Spelling in use*. Urbana, IL: National Council of Teachers of English

Levine, M. (2003). *The myths of laziness*. New York: Simon & Schuster.

Liberman, I.Y., Rubin, H., Duques, S., & Carlisle, J. (1985). Linguistic abilities and spelling proficiency in kindergarten and adult poor spellers. In D.B. Gray & J.F. Kavanagh (Eds.), *Biobehavioral measures of dyslexia* (pp. 163–176). Parkton, MD: New York Press.

Lyman, F. (1981). The responsive classroom discussion: The inclusion of all students. In A.S. Anderson (Ed.), *Mainstreaming Digest*. College Park: University of Maryland College of Education.

Marsh, G., Friedman, M., Welch, V., & Desberg, P. (1980). The development of strategies in spelling. In U. Frith (Ed.), *Cognitive processes in spelling* (pp. 339–353). New York: Academic.

McCracken, M., & McCracken, R. (1993). *Spelling through phonics*. Winnipeg, Manitoba, Canada: Peguis.

Moats, L. (1995). *Spelling: Development, disability and instruction*. Timonium, MD: York Press.

Morris, D. (1982). "Word sort": A categorization strategy for improving word recognition ability. *Reading Psychology, 3*, 247–259.

Moseley, D.V. (1997). Assessment of spelling and related aspects of written expression. In J.R. Beech & C. Singleton (Eds.), *The psychological assessment of reading*. London: Routledge.

Nagy, W., & Anderson, R.C. (1984). The number of words in printed school English. *Reading Research Quarterly, 19*, 304–330.

O'Brien, B. (1971). *Mrs. Frisby and the Rats of NIMH*. Canada: McClelland & Stewart.

Radebaugh, M.R. (1985). Children's perceptions of their spelling strategies. *The Reading Teacher, 38*, 532–536.

Ralston, M., & Robinson, G. (1997). Spelling strategies and metacognitive awareness in skilled and unskilled spellers. *Australian Journal of Learning Disabilities, 2*(4), 12–23.

Raths, L.E., Wasserman, S., Jonas, A., & Rothstein, A. (1986). *Teaching for thinking: Theory, strategies, and activities for the classroom*. New York: Teachers College Press.

Read, C., & Hodges, R. (1982). Spelling. In H. Mitzel (Ed.), *Encyclopedia of educational research* (5th ed., pp. 1758–1767). New York: Macmillan.

Rosencrans, G. (1993). *The effects of direct instruction within a whole language spelling program*. Unpublished master's thesis, Simon Fraser University, Vancouver, British Columbia, Canada.

Rosencrans, G. (1998). *The spelling book: Teach children how to spell, not what to spell*. Newark, DE: International Reading Association.

Rubeck, P. (1977). Decoding procedures: Pupil self-analysis and observed behaviours. *Reading Improvement, 14*, 187–192.

Schlagal, R.C. (1992). Patterns of orthographic development into the intermediate grades. In S. Templeton & D.R. Bear (Eds.), *Development of orthographic knowledge and the foundations of literacy* (pp. 31–51). Mahwah, NJ: Erlbaum.

Scott, J.A., Hiebert, E.H., & Anderson, R.C. (1992). Research as we approach the millennium: Beyond becoming a nation of readers. In F. Lehr & J. Osborn (Eds.), *Reading, language, and literacy: Instruction for the twenty-first century* (pp. 253–280). Hillsdale, NJ: Erlbaum.

Slavin, R.E. (1990). *Cooperative learning: Theory, research, and practice*. Englewood Cliffs, NJ: Prentice Hall.

Smith, F. (1988). *Joining the literacy club: Further essays into education*. Portsmouth, NH: Heinemann.

Snowball, D. (1996). Spelling strategies. *Instructor, 106*(1), 36–37.

Snowball, D. (1997). Spelling strategies. *Classroom, 17*(2), 20–21.

Stahl, S. (1992). Saying the "p" word: Nine guidelines for exemplary phonics instruction. *The Reading Teacher, 45*, 618–625.

Stiggins, R. (2002, January). Assessment FOR vs. assessment OF learning. *Tackle Box, 3*(1), 1.

Tarasoff, M. (1990). *Spelling strategies you can teach.* Victoria, British Columbia, Canada: Egan.

Templeton, S. (1992a). New trends in an historic perspective: Old story, new resolution—sound and meaning in spelling. *Language Arts, 69*(6), 454–463.

Templeton, S. (1992b). Theory, nature, and pedagogy of higher-order orthographic development in older students. In S. Templeton & D.R. Bear (Eds.), *Development of orthographic knowledge and the foundations of literacy* (pp. 253–275). Hillsdale, NJ: Erlbaum.

Templeton, S., & Bear, D.R. (1992a). *Development of orthographic knowledge and the foundations of literacy.* Mahwah, NJ: Erlbaum.

Templeton, S., & Bear, D.R. (1992b). A summary and synthesis: Teaching the lexicon to read and spell. In S. Templeton & D.R. Bear (Eds.), *Development of orthographic knowledge and the foundations of literacy* (pp. 333–351). Mahwah, NJ: Erlbaum.

Thomas, J.K. (1979). *Teaching spelling: Canadian word lists and instructional techniques.* Scarborough, Ontario, Canada: Gage Educational Publishing.

Thompson, R. (1930). The effectiveness of modern spelling instruction (Contributions to Modern Education, No. 436). New York: Columbia University Press.

Trieman, R. (1985). Onsets and rimes as units of spoken syllables: Evidence from children. *Journal of Experimental Child Psychology, 39*, 161–181.

Vygotsky, L.S. (1978). *Mind in society: The development of higher psychological processes* (M. Cole, V. John-Steiner, S. Scribner, & E. Souberman, Eds. & Trans.). Cambridge, MA: Harvard University Press. (Original work published 1934)

Westwood, P. (1999). *Spelling: Approaches to teaching and assessment.* Victoria, Australia: The Australian Council for Educational Research.

Wheatley, J. (2000). *Spelling instruction: Moving beyond word memorization in the intermediate grades.* Unpublished master's project, University of Victoria, British Columbia, Canada.

Wolf, D.E., Desberg, P., & Marsh, G. (1985, January). Analogy strategies for improving word recognition in competent and learning disabled readers. *The Reading Teacher, 38*, 412–416.

Wong, B.Y.L. (1986). A cognitive approach to teaching spelling. *Exceptional Children, 53*(2), 169–173.

Worthy, M.J., & Invernizzi, M. (1990). Spelling errors of normal and disabled students on achievement levels one through four: Instructional implications. *Bulletin of the Orten Society, 40*, 138–149.

Zutell, J. (1992). An integrated view of word knowledge: Correlational studies of the relationships among spelling, reading, and conceptual development. In S. Templeton & D.R. Bear (Eds.), *Development of orthographic knowledge and the foundations of literacy* (pp. 213–229). Hillsdale, NJ: Erlbaum.

Zutell, J. (1998). Word sorting: A developmental spelling approach to word study for delayed readers. *Reading and Writing Quarterly, 14*(2), 219–238.

in·dex

Note: Page numbers followed by *f, t,* and *r* indicate figures, tables, and reproducibles, respectively.